Twelve Steps to
Eighteen Holes

Twelve Steps to Eighteen Holes

LET GO, LET GOLF

Andrew Mecca, DrPH

California Mentor Foundation

Published by:

The California Mentor Foundation
100 Main Street, Tiburon, CA 94920
Tel: (415) 789-1007   Fax: (415) 789-1008 fax
www.calmentor.org

Visit us online at **www.12stepsto18holes.com**

ISBN: 978-0-9713680-4-0

Library of Congress Control Number: 2009905781

Front cover photo: © Stephen Morris, iStockphoto.com

Back cover photo: © Evan Schiller, golfshots.com

Cover and interior design: Gary Palmatier, Ideas to Images

Copyediting: Michael Mollett

Index: Medea Minnich

Printed in the United States of America.

Dedicated to Kate,

the love of my life,

from whom I have learned so much—
including her SECRETS for life,
shared in this book.

Contents

Foreword

By John Abendroth

This delightful book is a celebration of both the joy of golf and the satisfaction of good living. For pro golfers and amateur players alike, these chapters provide a unique perspective on what golf and life teach us about character.

Character and integrity are the true rewards of the spirit of competition. They easily surpass money, fame, endorsements, and trophy cases. Andy's little jewel of a book provides the key to honesty on the links and wholesomeness in life.

About Andy Mecca

I met Andy Mecca in 2002. Andy was chairing the Olympic Club Foundation that I had just joined. The foundation is dedicated to supporting athletic opportunities for young people throughout the Bay Area, and what struck me first was his friendliness and his commitment to young people. We also shared many similar interests, and delighted in talking about people we knew in common, causes we have each championed, and aspirations dear to our hearts.

What impressed me next about Andy was his fiercely healthy spirit of competition, the same drive that has powered my success in golf and life. Immediately, we became fast friends.

You may already know Andy as a much-esteemed leader in the world's recovery movement. He spent a decade, the '90s, as California's highly regarded drug czar, having been appointed by Governor Pete Wilson to revamp and revitalize the state's multipronged commitment to putting an end to substance abuse and building personal self-esteem.

Andy's competitiveness and discipline carry over into everything he does. He got into running in the '70s and was one of those who thought the more miles the better. Logging regular eighty-mile weeks, Andy ran in fifty marathons, did the Ironman, and then ran across America . . . twice.

Even though he did not start playing until he was fifty-five, he has done the same thing with golf. Picking up his first club at Hualalai, Hawaii, soon Andy was hitting a thousand balls and playing thirty-six holes a day.

So given Andy's career in the addictions field (and his personal addiction to golf), how appropriate that, in the pages of this book, he would draw on the wonderful Twelve Steps of personal recovery, and, with a bit of humor, apply the Twelve Steps to the wondrous game of golf's eighteen holes and all that they metaphorically represent in life.

Applying Golf's Lessons to Life

Twelve Steps to Eighteen Holes applies the insights of the Twelve Steps to what has come to be known as the futility of golf and, by extension, the powerlessness we frequently discover in our daily struggles off the golf course. Andy's wry humor and colorful storytelling clearly demonstrate how the lessons and triumphs we may achieve on the golf course spill directly into the same kinds of challenges we face in real life. In the voluminous literature of golf, I have never encountered this approach to both sport and life.

What is brilliant about Andy's book is that it shows how golf's challenges can enhance and elevate our performance in real life. If you show great character on the golf course by following the rules, keeping accurate score, and being a true gentleman and sportsman to your friends, then it is an easy transition to see how your life will improve where it truly counts—living each day with class, dignity, and integrity in the real world. In life and on the golf course, two frequently lonely excursions, character is what happens when nobody else is looking.

Drawing on Your Inner Strength

A great teacher gives the student the power to draw truth from within oneself. If my meager grasp of Latin is correct, the word *educate* means precisely that—"to draw from." Once that mechanism clicks in, there is no stopping the student. This is the power of Andy's book. It doesn't cover all the minute, highly detailed blueprints and golf lessons other golf books provide, but it does offer something much more powerful—the inspiration to help the reader love and like himself. That is probably the most addictive ingredient in life, one that is really, really hard to attain—the power of self-esteem.

Golf is a game of finesse. I love the sport for its ceaseless need for dedication and discipline. Come to think of it, any successful pursuit of worthwhile goals in real life simply cannot be attained without dedication and discipline, so it doesn't really matter whether you are sporting a bloodied football jersey or a *GQ* ensemble of golf's finest fashions. Without those fires that burn within and which come to fruition through the application of dedication and discipline, you may as well hang up your tattered jersey or retire your spiffy checkered golf slacks.

This book makes this pursuit fun and life enhancing. Andy helps you take a look at yourself without running in shame from the mirror. He makes golf even more exciting than it already is, and he makes our constant search for self-improvement both fun and attainable.

A Final Word on the American Spirit

I travel extensively across this great country, and I never get tired of meeting new friends. From my vantage point I watch with pride and admiration as Americans strive to improve their lot, keeping food on the table for their loved ones and creating fresh opportunities for their children to receive a quality education.

I firmly believe that our current financial crisis is also a wonderful growth opportunity. My fellow citizens have never run from a challenge, and I can tell you that Americans are not flinching now. I love them for this.

Who would have thought that a book about golf would be an instrument of the personal growth and social improvement we need these days? But that's how highly I regard Andy's book. It is a breezy, refreshing tool that will surprise you with its power to make you feel better as a person.

— John Abendroth, 2009

> John Abendroth is a native San Franciscan, a former PGA Tour player, and the course record holder (62) on the Lake course at the Olympic Club in San Francisco. He is the co-founder of Celtic Golf Management in San Francisco and the co-host, since 1994, of *Hooked on Golf* (Fox Sports Bay Area).

Preface

I've been working on this book, off and on, for some time now. Once in a while it will come up in conversation with my golfing buddies. Knowing me well, and not mincing words, they get right to the point, and ask:

What's the Point of This Book?

Good question. Is it a guide to improving your golf game? Can it help you be successful in your marriage? How about improving your career? Your personal life? I say yes to all of the above. I also say this book, in all its light-heartedness, can create a little bit more happiness in your life.

That's the overarching purpose. Happiness doesn't come easily in this often-crazy world. We aren't necessarily born with it. We certainly aren't given a guidebook to help us attain it. We are very capable of losing it; that's for sure. Happiness is elusive, baffling, fickle, complex, and sometimes seems downright impossible.

So you could say that my point is to lead you to a little bit of happiness. Happiness can be a fine addiction. Little ripples of joy help us forget and let go of the dark clouds of self-doubt and worry that hover above us way too long and serve only to impede our progress in life. Those same little ripples of joy expand and enrich our lives and the lives of those we love—and those who just happen to be nearby. If, by writing this book, I can spread a little happiness to people in places broader than my normal reach, that result more than justifies the time I've spent away from my loved ones—and from the golf course! And the process has been a wonderful outlet for me: I flat out love this game in all its forms, including writing (and talking) about it and its place in my universe. If I've succeeded in sharing my sheer awe of the pleasures in golf and the multitudinous ways in which golf can stand as a metaphor for so much in life, I'll consider it a good round.

Why Me?

Am I an expert on golf? Not by a long shot. Just ask any of my golfing partners. But I do firmly ascribe to what the golf great Arnold Palmer had to say about the game: "Golf is deceptively simple and endlessly complicated. It satisfies the soul and frustrates the intellect. It is at the same time rewarding and maddening. And it is without a doubt the greatest game mankind has ever invented." Consider *Twelve Steps to Eighteen Holes: Let Go, Let Golf* my homage to the game—and to more.

My qualifications to write this book come less from my skills on the course (sometimes debatable, often unpredictable) than from my professional life. In forty years of working in addiction recovery, youth recovery, and the youth development movement, I have been honored to work elbow to elbow with remarkably courageous, inspirational, and deeply committed people— adults and youths alike—who have helped make my life a constant stream of joy and revelation. To see change occur in a life that has been damaged, stalled, severely detoured, or deeply wounded is one of the most gratifying feelings a person can have. Making a difference to better the lot of a fellow human is really one of the loftiest meanings of life. To my way of thinking, helping another is at the core of what it means to be thoroughly human. A great lyric from the musical drama *Les Miserables* comes to mind: "To love another person is to see the face of God." For me, that sentiment, that goal, pretty well wraps up the meaning behind the phrase "a life well lived." If I discover nothing more in my entire time on earth than this, I'll have played my whole round smiling. To live well on the golf course and in life and spread that pleasure around? Now *that's* my idea of heaven.

What's Here?

Much of the structure of *Twelve Steps to Eighteen Holes: Let Go, Let Golf* is hidden in plain sight, right there in the title. I freely admit that golf can be an addiction. Does it need its own twelve-step program? See what you think as you read the book. And along the way, you'll enjoy some vicarious golf and a few stories, have some laughs, and have some insights about life along the way. Really, it's golf without the greens fees or the bag of clubs—and without needing to scan for lightning.

Each of the chapters (no surprise: there are twelve of them) includes a section I call Musings Between Holes, a more contemplative moment or two from the end of one hole to the beginning of another. And then, before each chapter's closing quotation from a wide range of golfing greats, there's The Secret. No, not *that* secret, but a tiny piece of the kaleidoscope of learnings, a little secret about the art of living that you, as a golfer, as a citizen, can impart to those coming up in your charge, either at your course or in your orbit.

The essence of secrets is that they aren't supposed to be told. In this case, I'd like to make an exception; actually, a lot of them. My secret, and one that I need to reveal right up front, is that most of these "secrets" are tips I've learned from my wife. They are based on the secrets she always shares with her students at the school she started in 1976 and has led since then. If they seem simple to you, you're right. Most are child-sized lessons, and easy enough—one at a time. It's the putting them together and into daily use that can take a lifetime of practice. Sounds like golf, doesn't it?

Much like your local golf pro who assesses your swing, then gives you a tip on how to improve your game, you can let these secrets flow into your game and let them work to enhance your life. Just as in Alcoholics Anonymous (AA), where the twelfth step is not really the final step, there's more after Chapter Twelve. There's an Epilogue and then a Nineteenth Hole—really a glossary of a few golfing terms and translations for life. So tee up, have some fun, and enjoy!

Acknowledgments

It would be impossible to even think of writing this book and sharing it with you without expressing my profound love and appreciation to all those who have encouraged me to take up the game of golf, who have mentored my game, who have shared generously by including me, and who have been a total pleasure in this golfing journey.

First and foremost are the Flanigans, who have encouraged me to play for decades; now we get to share numerous thrills with our golfing adventures.

To Bob Payne, Bill Price, Tom Callinan, John Hoskins, Ted Ward, Jerry Stratford, Bob Herwick, Mike House, Pat House, Mike Madden, Tom Akin, D. B. Murray, Mak Kariotis, Mike Reynolds, James Student, Xavier Burillo, Michael Stallone, Bo McCrum, and Gary Trono for sharing some of the most beautiful golf courses in the world and making possible some of my favorite rounds.

To my good friend Richard Kramer, with whom I have shared an annual pilgrimage to Pebble Beach and an occasional Saturday morning round at the Olympic Club. We have also golfed and shared other crazy adventures in New Zealand and beyond.

To all the guys at the Olympic Club—Chris Stein, Roger, Curtis—thanks again for your encouragement and coaxing to help me turn a tennis swing into a functional golf swing. And to Dick and Barbara Bechelli at the Olympic Club and in Hawaii.

To Rich Young and his infectious joy for golf and for the rounds at the Broadmoor before our Board meetings in Colorado Springs.

To all my friends at Hualalai, where I play 90 percent of my golf. To Rob Kildow, who has so generously shared journeys down to Hokuli'a with Chris Shilakes and me. Thanks to Rob and Pat, for the very animated Saturday morning matches and the hotly contested Nassaus that frequently end in ties.

To Bob, Ricci, Michael, and all the wonderful participants in the Tuesday afternoon "scramble," the regular Tuesday and Thursday skins games and all the very competitive tournaments.

To John Freitas who gave me my first lesson back in 2001. To Brendon, Jahn, Matt, Jake, Ken, Divo, and everyone at Hualalai who do so much to help make it fun and are a constant source of encouragement.

Heartfelt thanks also to the young men who work at the Hualalai courses and bring the spirit of aloha to each and every day on the range and on the course. This very special gang includes Iopa, Chad, Sam, and Chris at Ke'olu. On the Hualalai course, Brown Bear, Dennis, Hank, Stephen, Peter, Billy, Steve, Richard, and the ever-smiling Sid.

A special thanks to Benedict Coulter, who helped me cultivate the idea for this book and who is a joy to golf with, and to Lad and Rory Wilsey, who encouraged me from the beginning.

And I would be remiss not to share a special "thank you" to Debbie Schell, who invited me to play my first round of golf at Hualalai. She and her husband, Joe, have become dear friends and I will never forget Debbie for including me, despite the fact that I had no game, just plenty of enthusiasm about the game and about learning it.

Finally, much thanks to Peter Anderson and Jan Hunter for all their support in bringing this puppy to fruition and to Gary Palmatier for the cover and interior design, Mike Mollett for his meticulous editing, and Medea Minnich for her helpful index.

So as it is with life in general, it is the people who encourage us, share special experiences with us, and celebrate life's journey and our golfing adventures who make it all so fulfilling!

We're Powerless?

F OR VETERANS OF ALCOHOLICS ANONYMOUS (AA), ONE OF THE MORE vexing concepts to absorb arrives right at the very beginning, with Step One's whole notion of powerlessness. *Powerless.* It's at the very core of the very first of the Twelve Steps.* And look at that step. It's not just huge; it's colossal: *We admitted we were powerless over alcohol—that our lives had become unmanageable.*

Colossal, indeed. The word is closely connected to colossus (a statue of gigantic size and proportions) and hence to one of the seven wonders of the world: the Roman Colosseum, built nearly two thousand years ago. If you've been there—to Rome to see the Colosseum itself—or even if you've been in any of today's mammoth amphitheatres, you know how the enormity can take your breath away. How you can feel nearly microscopic beside something so massive.

More to the point, if you've faced an addiction of any sort, you know. You know overwhelming and huge. Even if you haven't, if your experience with addiction is all third-hand, chances are you know that alcoholics and addicts are fiercely strong-minded and extremely willful individuals. Powerless? Who'd have thought? It absolutely slays alcoholics and addicts to have to admit their powerlessness over their drug of choice. But until they do so, they will never free themselves from the fatal chains of addiction.

---

*All Twelve Step quotations are from Alcoholics Anonymous, *Alcoholics Anonymous: The Big Book*, 4th ed. (Alcoholics Anonymous World Services, 2001).

And much as I make light of the addiction to the game that comes over golfers, I know well what a negative addiction is. And how quickly and completely it can overtake an individual. I've seen it in settings and people all over the world. And in people whose backgrounds and circumstances absolutely defy the stereotypes of addiction.

Imagine, for example, a young soldier from the farm in Nebraska. Fresh faced, crew cut, polite, well-spoken, good at following orders. His commanding officer was thrilled when Derrick re-upped for a second tour. It was not until Derrick wound up in our hospital, severely addicted to heroin—China white heroin, 98 percent pure and unrelenting—that his real reasons became clear. Nineteen, maybe twenty when I first met him, Derrick was so deeply addicted that he had re-upped simply to stay where the drugs were plentiful and cheap—even if it meant continuing on as a rifle-carrying grunt, all too often in the Vietcong's gunsights. For Derrick, the heroin masked the overwhelming powerlessness he felt, living on the other side of the world, apart from all he knew, isolated from everyone he knew, left with the very clear knowledge of the danger that awaited out on patrol. Then he was left utterly powerless before an addiction that controlled every moment of his day. Despite his upbringing, despite his grounding, he had been at serious risk for addiction, probably from the moment he left the States. His was a perfect storm of powerlessness. Not something a farm boy—or a soldier—anticipates.

But golf? Who's powerless over golf? Is there anyone—anyone who has tried and been tempted by the game—who isn't? Hence the first of our steps:

> *We admitted that golf is so damn difficult that we have*
> *absolutely no power over our ability to do anything we want*
> *with our swing, our putting, our score, or, as a matter of fact,*
> *our very lives, lives we had hoped to enhance with a great*
> *day on the links.*

If we have no power, what do we have? How can we even start the day, let alone a round of golf, or a long-term goal of golfing well? Members of AA often rely on the phrase "Let go, let God." And in fact, they have no corner on the phrase. Google "Let go, Let God," or "Let go and let God," or any variation, and in a fraction of a second you'll have anywhere from eight million to eighty-four million possibilities. But in talking abut golf, how about simply this: Let go, let golf!

A side note to a factoid I discovered in writing the previous paragraph: even an episode from the first (and, it would seem, the last) season of the 2007 television show "In Case of Emergency" was called "Let Go, Let Golf." Not something I've seen. But, in the course of this book, I will tell a few stories of the upside I've seen and felt in using the phrase myself—and encouraging others to do the same.

"I Get My Strength from Powerlessness." Who Knew?

If one of the keys to overcoming addiction is powerlessness, where else does this key work? Turns out, golf and life are also about powerlessness. Where does the courage come from to think such audacious thoughts as even attempting to drill a ball into thin air against insurmountable physical odds and have it spike like a dart next to (or even in!) a tiny hole thousands of feet away? In life, how do we summon the courage to lace our shoes each morning when so many hazards of daily living howl in our faces like wind-driven golf flags laughing at our plight? How do we succeed when we are basically powerless? That is the ultimate question about life, golf, and addiction.

Powerless. When you think about all the things that can possibly go wrong, it's a wonder we attempt the sport at all. A golf swing is perhaps the oddest of all athletic functions. We wield a club, which we try to make an extension of our limbs, smoothly functioning with our very imperfect bodies. We strive to mesh all the movable parts of our physiques into a symphonic testament to discipline so that the ball can be struck cleanly, squarely, and with a high degree of power and accuracy.

Powerless. Consider the external physical properties of our endeavor. Maybe we are teeing off early in the morning. Perhaps it's foggy, drizzly, and cold. Maybe the wind is sporadic and unpredictable. Sometimes the elements are so fickle there's not much even a perfectly crafted swing can do to combat Mother Nature. And, oh yeah, there you are perched above a tiny ball, hoping to demolish it cleanly while—and here's the greatest challenge—the planet on which you are standing is spinning furiously and wildly through its orbit. Okay, that last challenge is a bit far-fetched, but I did watch a playing partner once whiff a tee shot entirely. When asked what happened, he smiled sheepishly and said: "Frankly, guys, when you consider that the Earth is spinning and I have a killer hangover, I think I came pretty damn close!" We gave him a mulligan. (A *mulligan*? The back of the book includes a glossary of definitions for any nongolfers and a sampling of golf giggles, for those who are looking for a few extra laughs.)

There is an absolutely wonderful paragraph in the book *The Legend of Bagger Vance,* by Steven Pressfield. Absorb the words. "The path of beating balls defeats the player, as it must, until he surrenders at last and allows his swing to swing itself. The path of study and dissection leads only to paralysis, until the player likewise surrenders and allows his overloaded brain to set down its burden, till in empty purity it remembers how to swing."

Imagine it. Imagine the pure freedom of just allowing your "swing to swing itself." In golf and in life. For now, I invite you to think about golf in that way. Take it easy, for a day, for a round, and see how it works. Golf is such an all-embracing arena of difficulty that the overloaded mind can easily become the player's worst nightmare. Instructional books and videos too numerous to count are legendary for the litany of physical drills, drills that then flood golfers' minds as they prepare themselves for the sport.

Serious golfers setting themselves up for the shot are a sight to behold. You can almost see the checklist of mental drills sparking from their minds. Their body language is a severely coiled intricacy of wiggles, waggles, clenching, tightening, loosening, swiveling of hips, wriggling of toes. Just to watch them in action can be exhausting.

Let go of all those checklists and corrections. Approach the ball. Breathe deeply. Feel good about the day. Strike the ball. Feel good about yourself as that tiny little golf ball splits the fairway in half. Put your driver back in the bag and start walking. Breathe deeply. Feel good. Repeat, changing the club as appropriate. Stroke that ball right into the cup.

Musings Between Holes

Golfers know these musings well. They are the moments between lifting one's ball out of the cup and completing the trek toward the next tee. Sometimes the walk is brief; sometimes it is a twisting, visually pleasing little hike through hillocks, over creeks, past lakes. This interval in golf's unending drama has always fascinated me. Sometimes fellow players use the time to comment—no, complain—about the preceding hole; often the time is spent in small talk, gossip, or boasting.

I like to think of these moments as clearing experiences for the mind, cleansing moments for the soul. A chance to breathe deeply, without focusing on the ball. Or that tiny little cup at the end. We will take these walks together in each of the Twelve Step chapters. With luck, we'll learn some things about being better players and, more importantly, being better people.

My wife used to always be amazed when I'd come home from golfing with some friends and I couldn't answer her questions about how my friends are, how their kids are, how work is—basic stuff. My response that "we talked about GOLF" left her shaking her head. After untold hours on the course and years of her disbelief, I have made more of an effort to check in on a more personal level. I now get some of the important details of how life is going. I've found that the golf course gives plenty of opportunity for conversations about life—and I do feel more enriched by these interactions. That's not to say that Golf Talk doesn't happen—I still love talking golf and all that goes with it, including the banter. Fact is, I love *all* the conversations walking a golf course.

There is something disarming about sharing a round of golf and the conversations that emerge on the course and afterward. I have a regular Saturday morning round with two friends, Rob and Pat, that includes some unabashed banter, trash talking over the $5 Nassau, and constant expressions of sheer joy for this shared time. This is all part of the total golf experience that I so love and appreciate getting to participate in now and forever.

The Secret

As I mentioned in the Preface, the essence of secrets is that they aren't supposed to be told. But the secrets at the end of each of these chapters are secrets that could benefit all of us, so why not cast them broad and wide? In fact, generations of children have learned most of these secrets early on, in my wife's school. Still more of us have picked them up along the way. And, at least in my mind, they all warrant consideration and refreshers, throughout life.

Think of these as little nuggets of truth that can enhance your life. And unlike the nuggets about the mechanics of your golf game that your local golf pro doles out after assessing your swing, these secrets won't leave you paralyzed above the ball. You don't have to think about your grip, or your feet, or your swing. Just let these secrets work to improve your game, in life.

As I've learned in forty years of working in the youth recovery and development movement, and considerably fewer years on the golf course and the practice green, helping (and being helped) requires honesty. Honest words; honest actions. On the small scale of the golf course, had I stuck only to the golf banter and not opened my ears and heart to more, my life and the ripples I have made would have been entirely different. I try, in my actions and in this book, to pass on some of the secrets and tips, many of which (just as in my golf game) I've learned (and sometimes relearned) the hard way, over time.

The first secret? *Be honest.* Now how hard is that? No harder than the perfect golf game.

Growth, growth toward honesty, starts with truthful acknowledgment about who you are, where you are, what you are feeling. You don't always have to be the one who casts the happy smile in the room, the person most eager to please. Embrace your humanity, because it's *all* of you that is worth giving. Some of the most engaging characters I've met on the golf course are those struggling, coarse-spoken, mumbling—and lovable—personalities who show all their faults and some of their virtues with each swing. The more vulnerable you are, the more eager will be the Gods of Golf to lift you from misery into occasional glory.

And, yes, just like golf, honesty requires practice. Practice, practice, practice. The good news is you can practice every day, every moment, through all kinds of weather. Which takes me to the first of a series of quotes to live, and golf, by. With one obvious exception—trust me, you'll know it when you see it—these are all from championship golfers or champion golf writers.

> *"One of the most fascinating things about golf is how it reflects the cycle of life. No matter what you shoot, the next day you have to go back to the first tee and begin all over again and make yourself into something."*
>
> — Peter Jacobsen

2

S T E P   T W O

Golf Can Restore Us?

W**HAT'S THIS? THE LAST CHAPTER TALKED THROUGH THE POWER OF** powerlessness and then wound up with a quotation about having to start all over again, every day. Every day? Don't people gather quotations that are uplifting? This one could be crazy-making.

Ah yes, now it's time for the second of AA's twelve steps: *Came to believe that a Power greater than ourselves could restore us to sanity.*

Sanity. You're interested in sanity, and you've chosen to play golf? How many comedy sketches have been played out on that one? It's never-ending fodder for comedians and frustration for golfers. Surely you know how hard the game is, physically and mentally. And now you want to bring sanity into it? Time for another step:

> *We came to believe that only something Powerful and outside of ourselves—the friendship of our golfing partners, the shared humor, the allure of the nineteenth hole, the comfort of a good meal, or some combination of all of these—could restore us to sanity and bring us to that inevitable moment when we sigh and murmur to anyone who might care what we think, "Well, it's great to be outside, isn't it?"*

Let go, let golf.

On bad days on the golf course, it absolutely pays to look on the bright side, to reframe the situation and lighten the load. As I remind myself after a bogey (or worse), if that outrageous slice is all I have to worry about, the world's okay. After all, there I am, amid the peaceful landscape of a golf course; why not enjoy the sounds of nature, and the day?

The Power of Numbers

In contrast, the clinic I ran in Long Bien, Vietnam, was an intense place, on many levels. Golf was not even on my radar back then. My job was to help soldiers as they battled their addictions. Remember: many of these were addictions to 98 percent pure China white heroin. Powerful stuff, much more powerful than anything anyone might find stateside. The soldiers were isolated. We all were isolated. And what would they go back to once they were clean? Another battle out in Vietnam, with the prospect of death or maiming just around the next bend. And what future if they made it home? Certainly not a hero's welcome stateside. Few people who understood what they'd been through. Maybe only few prospects for a job.

Think about these questions too long, and the soldiers' choice to anesthetize themselves against the horrors of war start to look a little different. As if it weren't enough to treat addicted soldiers, we were trying to help them detoxify while the horrific situations they'd just left were still front of mind. And might yet be their next assignment. It was *M*A*S*H* without the methodical comfort of medicine and the predictability of physical wounds healing. We were dealing with psychic wounds, raw fear, abandonment, isolation. The chemical addictions were simply the presenting problem. Powerful stuff, all to be fixed in military order, within the condensed time frame of war.

That context explains, in part, how it was that Derrick went from being completely strung out on heroin to counseling the next batch of soldiers behind him. Very competently, and within just a few weeks of the throes of his addiction. After a horrific period of detox and counseling—counseling in which he shared his utter loneliness, his fears of soldiering in Vietnam, and his potential future back in the states—Derrick learned and took to heart the lessons people often take years, even decades, to discover. It is, to my mind, the collective discovery of AA, and the premise upon which any twelve-step program is built: I'm not alone. In getting through the brutal physical effects of withdrawal from drugs, sharing his fears with the counselors and the other addicts, Derrick saw that his deepest fears were not his alone. He saw that he had been side by side with soldiers who felt just the same, and to whom heroin had also become the perfect shield. That is, until it became their demon. In working through his addiction, he discovered a community, a bond, a tribe. All in military double time.

Those of us running the clinic faced our own kinds of fear and stress. We were under the microscope, carving new ground. Not only did we have to help these soldiers, and quickly, we were constantly watched. By congressional delegations, by the media. The stress levels ratcheted up sky-high, for a host of reasons. I was twenty-three years old, in charge of building, staffing, supplying, and running two hospitals and, over time, an additional fourteen rehab centers, in different locations. How sane was that?

I can tell you that what sanity I maintained was derived in major part from an addiction that took hold of me there. Running. I found that running cleared my head, the endorphins made me feel good, and soon those runs became longer and longer. By my calculations, I was running one hundred miles a week in those days, easily. Often, I was running fifteen to twenty miles a day. The terrain was safe enough. The lake I looped around was blissfully serene and practically dead center of the military installation's huge acreage. At that point, my running seemed a sane answer to the pressures around me. My days had three parts, often repeated: sleep, run, work. My pattern was in direct contrast to the man next door, who kept his humor, his sanity, and a radiant calm, without ever lacing up a running shoe, breaking a sweat, or even breaking open a bottle.

In Happy Places, This Is How We Do It

There was an orphanage right next door to the hospital in Long Bien. The Buddhist monk who ran the place was as calm as I was frenetic. And his was not an easy job. He was responsible for the safety and well-being of an ever-growing group of babies and children who had been abandoned by their mothers, left on the doorstep. These children—their mothers, Vietnamese; their fathers, American GIs—were *con lai*, half-breeds, and in that culture, the word said a lot. Beyond their mixed heritage, and often because of it, they were most often abandoned, in complete poverty, and considered untouchables by the mainstream culture. The children were referred to as *bui doi*, translated as "the dust of life," a term used for the poorest of the poor. The American government, especially in the early years of the engagement, didn't recognize the issues or the enormity of this growing population.

The monk, Master Vin, had his hands full, literally and figuratively, running the orphanage on a shoestring. And always, rather than being run down or debilitated by the demands on him, his unfailing flow of positive attitude was energizing for him and for those around him. His laughter was rich, full, and frequent. He could find something to laugh at and someone to laugh with—no matter what the circumstance. Often, his laughter stemmed from the humor he found in human behavior, even in what the rest of us might think of as dramatic, tense moments. Or at least what I saw that way.

One day I happened to be over at the orphanage just as a woman came in, already in labor. A little-used aspect of my training in the medical service corps kicked in—just enough to have me a bit frantic. Master Vin saw my face as I mentally ran down the list of equipment we'd need and things to do to help this woman, and scrambled off to prepare. "Andy," he called after me, "Come back. Relax. Just wait." Sure enough, within minutes, the mother-to-be squatted down and, as Master Vin smiled and spoke to her quietly, promptly gave birth—to her fifth child. As he tended to the mother and baby, he looked over at me and said, "See? In happy places, this is how we do it."

Happy places? My clinic was not a happy place, not by a long stretch. But his orphanage? Yes, despite the hardship, despite the children's circumstances, it was. He ran the place with extraordinary calm and with energy perfectly suited to any occasion that arose. Against all odds, his was a safe, nurturing home for a generation of children.

In that moment, as he and the mother smiled at me, I couldn't help but laugh—at myself and in relief. Mine wasn't the same as one of his deep, rollicking belly laughs, laughs that filled the lungs and—as he had explained to me many times—were good for the human body. My laugh may not have released peptides and increased my immunity as he'd assured me good laughter could, but it was a start. And it nudged me much closer to understanding and believing his adage that we're at our best when we're laughing. Truth be told, my newfound addiction to running and the lessons I learned from Master Vin were what kept me on track through my experience in Vietnam.

My life these days is a long way from the clinic in Vietnam, but the lessons and the laughter continue to be laced throughout. Most days, Master Vin comes along with me, coaching me in my head, helping me find the laughter. He would find great humor in how much time we spend walking golf courses, chasing after a tiny little white ball.

Musings Between Holes

If you haven't figured it out by now, know that golf is a passion of mine. It is for many of my friends as well. It's not just the game itself that fascinates us, but it's also what happens after—even as—we struggle, compete, and play together. I can compare it to the kind of endorphin release long-distance runners experience at the end of their journey; the feeling of euphoria or "being in the zone" comes close to describing what occurs after a convivial round of golf. Having run fifty marathons and two cross-country runs (across the width of the United States, not just over hill and dale), and competed in the

Ironman Triathlon, my knees won't tolerate running any longer. Happily, I can still carry my bag for thirty-six holes, and it is sheer joy. Do I miss running? Sure. For one thing, I wish I could still run so I could join one of the young stud pros at Hualalai Resort in Kona, Jahn, who plays speed golf—for fun. He plays nine holes with a driver, an iron, a wedge, and a putter. But there's more: he does it in under thirty minutes—and plays even. Maybe, maybe in my running days I could have done the under thirty minutes part. But the even part? I'm still dreaming.

The reality is that my friends and I are hard-working, conscientious citizens who have labored long and hard in careers that we like to think are community-oriented and life-enhancing. Golf affords us the chance to display our individual skills in a communal setting. I could not come close to adequately describing the joys of friendship that golf provides—the bonds we've secured over the years; the deep, mutual, abiding care we show toward each others' families and vocations; the moments of hilarity that spring from the spontaneity of the sport; the intergenerational celebration of athleticism, food, libation, and friendship.

We are serious-minded about having fun, serious about supporting each other, and, man, are we organized! One of my favorite golf experiences occurred a few years ago. Not surprisingly, it involved one of my closest friends for fifty years, Jack Flanigan. Jack and I were best friends growing up; he helped talk me into running the clinic in Vietnam, back when he was running a hospital in Cam Ranh Bay. I can't help but wonder if part of the reason wasn't hidden in his request to me, before I left the States, to be sure to bring extra tennis balls. We've played many sports together over the years, and I've felt a part of his family through all those games and all those years.

So as Jack approached that big milestone of 6-0, I asked if he wanted a big party. His answer? Absolutely NOT. Okay then, what did he want instead? He was the first of our small group to turn sixty and there was no way we'd let the birthday pass unnoticed. What he wanted seemed like a fantasy, a pipe dream. He wanted to have his brothers and all their sons take an extended golf holiday in Carmel. Luckily for me, he counted me as one of his Flanigan brothers; as the social chairman of this group, I started planning something worthy of this life experience.

We started on Wednesday morning at Cypress. It was all the wonder a golfer could hope for. This was followed by an afternoon round at Spyglass and a personal record (a best round) for two of us. We had fun (but not great scores) at Poppy the next day. Then we played the Preserve, sponsored by a dear friend, James Student. Ours were the three foursomes on the course on Friday; we decided this truly was a heavenly experience. We then moved into the Lodge at Pebble Beach to play Spanish Bay on Saturday and finish big at Pebble on Sunday.

What an extraordinary golfing experience. But even better was the sharing and storytelling of fifty years as an extended family. Best of all, for me, was having the sons of the Flanigan brothers each come up and say thank you for giving them one of the best gifts of all. Certainly, the courses and the golf were great, but what they most enjoyed was the extended opportunity to gain insights into their dads' and their uncles' remarkable lives.

The stories could be a book unto themselves. But the end of our round at Spanish Bay gives a glimpse. We finished at 6 p.m., just as the bagpipes started skirling. Jack (every bit the Irishman) was amazed and overcome, so touched that someone at the course knew it was his birthday. How could they have known this would be the perfect way to help him celebrate his day? Jack was so thrilled, I didn't have the heart to say otherwise—right then.

The Secret

So it is with golf and special golfing experiences: we play, we toast, we laugh, we breathe deep gasps of gratitude, we celebrate! And in the process, we bolster our own sanity as individuals, we bolster each other, and we see the power of friendship. Again and again. And these friendships—among family, peers, and across generations—link us to a much broader web in the world.

And so, we come to the second secret: *Golf is a ritual of friendship*. For some, it's an exercise in frustration; for some it's a career. For the rest of us, what keeps us coming back—more than the addiction, more than the elusive promise of a perfect round—is the feeling of connection we find with our golfing friends.

In my life, I have never found a game, a sport, a match, or an activity that lends itself to a celebration of life more than golf. Golf is a vehicle for the celebration of friendship. What keeps me fueled for life's other, more serious-minded responsibilities and career demands are the regular, ongoing, memorable occasions that serve as venues for my mantra: *Always celebrate*. When I think about the ritualistic celebration of golf, I am reminded of T. S. Eliot's words in the *Four Quartets*, "Little Gidding":

> *We shall not cease from exploration*
> *And the end of all our exploring*
> *Will be to arrive where we started*
> *And know the place for the first time.*

For me, these words take on a different meaning on the golf course.

To fully appreciate the course and its challenges, our friends and our celebrations, in golf and in life, we do need to approach every day, every occasion, and every obstacle with fresh eyes. And with laughter, as the next quote emphasizes:

> *"There is no other sport that gives us so many opportunities to*
> *laugh with our friends. The game can be so absurd at times that*
> *laughter is the only thing that keeps us from going insane . . .*
> *The laughter reminds us that no matter how solitary our pursuit,*
> *we are never truly alone in our frustration."*
>
> — Gary Player

Let It Go and Play

FOR THOSE USING THE TWELVE STEPS TO OVERCOME ADDICTION OF any variety, this next step can be a major leap. Consider the third step: *Made a decision to turn our will and our lives over to the care of God as we understood Him.*

Now *that's* a big one: turning our will and our lives over. Addiction may have turned our lives inside out, but this takes it a step further. Turning our will and our lives over to someone or something we can't see, we can't prove is there? Whoa. But, remember, this is one step at a time, or, as the bumper sticker says, "One Day at a Time."

If it can't be one day at a time, what about one morning at a time? One round at a time? One hole at a time? One stroke at a time? What about simply not overthinking your golf game? What about just letting go? Letting go and letting golf?

So here's our next step:

> We made a decision to give up caring what our swing looks like, what our ultimate score might be, what our golfing friends might think of our wardrobe, who would be buying drinks in the clubhouse, and, frankly, everything we thought we ever knew about golf. After all, these greens fees are mighty expensive. How about we let golf take care of us for a change.

Let go, let golf.

Lee Trevino: The Perfect Model
for Letting Go, Letting Golf

I cannot think of a more ideal role model for how to approach golf—and life—than Lee Trevino. Known as "The Merry Mex" or "Super Mex," Trevino brought joy, irreverence, panache, and uniqueness to a game that was, in his time, becoming an overly serious endeavor mastered by lackluster characters carved from cookie-cutter golf schools.

Trevino did not fit the mold, and neither did his game. Raised in poverty in Texas, where he worked as a child in the cotton fields, Trevino started caddying at age eight. He quickly began taking every opportunity to practice at the courses, day and night. He even found ways to golf during his service in the Marine Corps, and he did so in an official capacity, playing in tournaments for the Marines when he extended his enlistment. Soon he became good enough to start challenging established players. Part street hustler, part stand-up comedian, Trevino spawned so many stories about playing—and winning—with a Dr Pepper bottle that they seem apocryphal. But sure enough, in his autobiography, *They Call Me Super Mex,* he wrote that the Dr Pepper bottle was one of his most famous gimmick bets—and that he "played with that bottle for three years and never lost to someone playing with a club." The backstory, that he also told, is that he practiced (imagine it: practicing with a family-size soda bottle) for nearly a year before taking his new gimmick public. Only Trevino.

He joined the PGA Tour in 1967, won the U.S. Open in 1968 at Oak Hill in Rochester, New York, and put together an impressive string of twenty-nine regular PGA victories (including six majors) and twenty-nine Champions Tour wins (including four majors). Forever chattering and cackling on greens and fairways, constantly playing to adoring galleries, Trevino was a working-man's hero who golfed with abandon, fearlessness, creativity, imagination, and a very sober sense of who he was in a drama co-starring the supreme likes of Arnold Palmer, Jack Nicklaus, and Gary Player.

Boiled down to bare bones, Trevino's approach was stark and simple: come to the tee whistling and joking, eschew all practice swings, wisecrack to the gallery, and hit away. He was a joy to watch. His style often rankled other players—he once pulled a rubber snake out of his golf bag and chased down Jack Nicklaus!—but his love of the sport and life itself endeared him to golf fans everywhere.

It seemed, however, that Mother Nature was not a fan when, in 1975, lightning struck Trevino. Of course, on a golf course (the thirteenth green, of all places); of course, during a tournament—the Western Open. Later, Trevino joked about it—he joked about everything—but the damage to his spine also hurt his game. That is, until he reinvented his swing and got back his championship game. And only Trevino can joke about lightning strikes, saying: "If you are caught on a golf course during a storm and are afraid of lightning, hold up a 1-iron. Not even God can hit a 1-iron."

Classic Trevino, master of the ability to keep it light and keep it fun. That ability to let go and enjoy is something to be nourished. And if a professional golfer can do that, why not the rest of us? After all, we're not making money playing the game—and, frustrating though it may be, golf is a *game*. A hard game, often an impossibly hard game, but a game.

Just Play Golf!

When I need to be reminded to not take myself or my game seriously, I replay any of a range of John Madden's quips and stories in my head. Madden, the famous football broadcaster and former head coach of the Oakland Raiders, looks like a mountain and, with those brooding eyebrows, can project a somewhat menacing visage. But he has a self-deprecating sense of humor and is delightfully childlike, supremely playful when it comes to laughing at himself. If you've heard him, you know what I mean. Here's just one example, a snippet that I caught recently on his morning radio show. He was talking about a discovery he had just made concerning his golf game.

I gotta tell ya, I have decided not to keep score when I play golf. It's great! I have never played better or enjoyed it more. The secret is I just don't care anymore. It's like the weight of the world is off my shoulders. We live in such a competitive world that the whole idea of beating my partners was overwhelming any other reasons to play. It was making me a really bad player, so I just decided not to keep score anymore.

Now you have to understand that there are few people as competitive as I am. The idea of losing kills me. So, in one dramatic step, I removed that instrument of pain. I simply don't score. *I just play golf.* All the things I used to love about the game are coming back to me—the joy of being outside, the satisfaction of making a great shot every now and then, the companionship of good friends.

Think about it. If you are at all competitive in life, you are constantly trying to be at the top of your game in whatever field you are in. Life teaches us that if you work hard enough and apply yourself, you will eventually "get it" and move on to the next challenge. This is true of most careers and almost all sports. Golf is the exception. We never really "get it" to the point of conquering it. And pity the poor fool who has a great day on the links and thinks he has arrived. The game will bite him in the butt the next time he plays.

The only possible exception I can think of is Tiger Woods. His achievements have been supernatural, but what you have to realize about him is that he is never satisfied. Never. He says there will always be more to accomplish, more changes to make. And he is his greatest critic. That's his secret. For the rest of us mortal souls, the secret, I believe, is simply to surrender to the game, not try to conquer it. By doing so, the game will show us things we never dreamed of experiencing. (John Madden, *The Daily Madden*, KCBS Radio.)

There you have it. The words from the Big Guy fairly well sum up what I am trying to achieve in *Twelve Steps to Eighteen Holes: Let Go, Let Golf.* Granted, I don't believe the decision to play without a scorecard is going to catch on like an epidemic, especially given the homage players devote to golf's sacred traditions. But . . . maybe the whole idea of surrender, genuine relaxation, and letting go just might gain some traction. And who knows? Maybe your golf game will improve. Maybe your outlook on life will take on a more mellow rhythm. And perhaps your marriage and relationships will deepen and mature.

In a sport best known for being the showcase of the impossible, maybe the very act of surrendering to its toughness will make possible sweeter things in your daily life. Let's tee it up and see.

Actually, let's tee up and see—in a different way. Trevino played golf at night when he was first learning, in part to avoid the groundskeepers and the fee takers. Exactly how he made that work I don't know, but I suspect it had a lot to do with his relaxed attitude and his love of the game. But it wasn't until recently that I, too, discovered some of the freedom that comes with night golf. Now, I'm not advocating that you slip onto a course under cover of darkness; in fact I absolutely don't recommend that. But if ever you have the chance to play sanctioned night golf, give it a try. For three nights during the year (around Christmas, Easter, and the Fourth of July), the Hualalai course on the Big Island of Hawaii sets up for night golfing, lining five holes with glow sticks. Whenever our niece Scarlett and her best friend, Paige, are with us then, *this* is how they want to golf. The tee boxes, the fairways, and the greens are lined with glow sticks. The pin itself glows in the dark. It makes for a slightly phosphorescent outline of a few holes of golf. And, truly, it's magical. You can't see the hazards, you can't see the trees, and some nights you can't even see your clubs or your feet. Luckily, you've been given a glow-in-the-dark golf ball, so you can see that—at least when you tee up. If your sight line is clear and your vision is good, you *might* see the pin, off in the distance. There is no choice: you have to let go, let golf. With fewer visual distractions and fewer visual cues, you have to just *play*. Visualize contact with the ball, visualize that perfect arc, visualize the ball dropping into the hole, and just enjoy the game. Complaining simply can't enter into it; after all, under these conditions, no one expects to do well. It's all for the pure enjoyment of it. The way it's played at Hualalai, it's unfailingly upbeat and positive. You play the best ball (and there's a pro in every foursome), so everyone gets a great game. Could there be a better way to pass on the joy of the game? To remind yourself of the pure pleasure to be had while golfing? To enjoy a night under the stars, a walk in the open air? And to let go, let golf?

Musings Between Holes

Scarlett, Paige, and night golfing have taught me a lot about golf. Through that and years of golfing with a wide-ranging cast of adolescents, teens, and young adults, I've come to see golf as both a metaphor for life and as an unparalleled opportunity for transmitting the skills and the presence that people can rely on all their lives. Golf provides constant opportunities to model and mentor—to be a role model—opportunities to help instill important character traits. To instill traits, such as patience and perseverance, that help improve one's game and, more importantly, improve one's life—one game, one day, and one life at a time. Be open to the possibilities, and you can glimpse the magic that can happen on the golf course, with family, with friends, and across generations. And the sharing—of skills, of knowledge, of life lessons—that can happen through golfing is a gift.

Golf has a myriad of gifts and pleasures to offer. Good thing, too, for it has just as many frustrations. On both sides of that, the opportunities for lessons are enormous and endless. What better vehicle than golf to pass on some of life's hardest lessons, safely and within a supportive community? As children watch their parents or other adults struggle mightily with the toughest sport on Earth, they see ways of tackling new challenges. They learn. We can hope they learn positive, healthy, constructive ways to golf and to live. And by working with them, we can do more than simply hope.

The Secret

Although sometimes it seems as though teenage ears are shut, they hear everything—and they see everything. It takes awareness and time to pass on some of the lessons we've learned, to help others avoid mistakes we may have made. But it doesn't take any more time to pass on the right lessons than the wrong ones. Why not take that step to play it forward, to help that next generation, whether it's your own children, others' children, or both? After all (and I'm calling it a secret, but it's not): *Children are our greatest gifts—and our time is the greatest gift to them.*

Even if you don't have children or don't have daily interactions with children in your work or community, you can have an enormous effect. Even if only a fraction of your words fall on young ears, your words and—more significantly—your actions can speak volumes. You may not see the ripple effect of walking your talk in the moment, and may not know it in the long-term. But your behavior—on the golf course, in the course of your life—is seen and may well be imitated. And in the long view, what lasts is not the mechanics of your golf stroke but what you bring to the game, the attitude you present, and how you deal with all the shots, good and bad, on the course and in life. Why not shake off the bad shots, appreciate the good, and celebrate the game and the friendships? Why not enjoy it and play it forward? And as you play it forward, remember that by putting the bad shots behind you, you can better see the good ahead of you.

> *"Sometimes things work out on the golf course and sometimes they don't. Life will go on. You try to understand what happens, but maybe today I don't want to know. I just screwed up, so maybe I should just put it behind me."*
>
> — Greg Norman

Inventory Time

*H*AVING MADE THE LEAP WITH STEP THREE, THE FOURTH OF AA'S Twelve Steps seems much more down to earth. The step? *Made a searching and fearless moral inventory of ourselves.* An inventory is one thing; a moral inventory is harder. And then, the requirement to make it searching and fearless adds a dimension to the inventory that demands significant work. But still, it's an inventory. Got to be a finite list.

But with golf? Where do you stop?

> *We vowed to make a searching and fearless moral inventory of our addiction to golf and to consider all the questions that arise. Why are we doing this? What do we hope to attain? How do we want to feel at the end of a long, torturous day of trying to sink that little ball? What life lessons have we learned after a day on the links? Honestly, are we better people after the eighteenth hole than we were when we teed off on the first hole? How about after the nineteenth hole?*

And, just as important as any of the questions just asked, what influence did you, as an individual, have on the rest of your foursome? On others on the course? On those you left in the morning and those you'll return to later? Is your golf addiction serving you well? What about its impact on others in your life?

Can you put those questions in the back of your head to percolate while you let go, let golf?

Ripples Out

There's a current television commercial that starts with one person doing a small kindness for another, a stranger on the street. Then that kindness gets passed on: the first stranger notices a fresh opportunity and makes a small act that brightens the immediate moment for yet another stranger. The idea of that positive ripple moving out to an ever-increasing group, of one small action ultimately lifting a sea of people always brings a smile to my face.

Will it make me buy the product? Maybe not. But it does remind me how one small action can quickly multiply. And, yes, this is one reason that I consciously make my enjoyment of the game—and my pleasure in those glorious, ritualized moments before and after—visible, to myself and to others. I know it lifts me up, and I hope it does others, as well.

Can Golf Teach You to Be a Little Happier in Your Life?

While we're thinking of ripples, I want to give you a fun mental exercise. I am going to list some of the sensory joys I gain from a round of golf, as well as some of the character-building opportunities that the sport affords. Simply see if any or all of these apply to your daily life. If so, and if you haven't already, maybe you can adapt and shape these things into your life away from golf. I promise you these are fun steps that can lead to the attainment of happiness, that ever-elusive source of joy that can pump new life into our veins.

It starts with getting out of the car in the golf course parking lot. While changing into your golf shoes as you perch on the bumper of your car or sit in the locker room, you exchange pleasantries with fellow golfers as they pass by and greet you warmly. There is a sense of newness, excitement, and possibility in the crisp morning air. There is also something strangely musical about the scraping of spikes on asphalt, the clanging of golf clubs in their bags as players begin their trek to the first tee.

Near the clubhouse, you fetch a couple of balls from your bag and join your friends on the practice green. This is a great way to get into the flow and feel of the day. Limber up, exchange pleasantries, relax, and breathe deeply. This is a new day, a fresh start, a clean canvas.

Make mental notes to yourself about what you are trying to achieve. Golf is not just about the bloodlust for sheer domination. It is the best sport known to man that offers the individual the chance to display fair play, gracious sportsmanship, and rigorous honesty. Golf also affords easy interpersonal situations in which you can showcase your social skills. Share pieces of your life with your friends. Inquire about their lives, their families, their hopes and wishes. Let the competition of the match and the energies attained spill over into your personality. One complements the other. Reflect on who you are in a hurly-burly world that all too seldom offers the fun, playful ways to express yourself that the game of golf can provide.

Be aware that people are watching you. Don't be vain about it. Or self-conscious. Be humble. Take a moment to call upon all the loftier regions of your soul. There is nothing like golf to help you practice the deep virtues of character demonstrated in fairness, scrupulous honesty, and the generous and sincere praise of others. We are all works-in-progress. Use golf as a vehicle to better yourself as an ever-evolving person.

Your behavior, your actions make an impression on people far more than your words. Be disciplined and rigorous when it comes to golf etiquette. Be aware that your actions do create a ripple effect; it's your choice, for good or for bad. If you are conscientious in your actions, you will see equally conscientious actions in others.

Replace your divots when your shot raises chunks of fairway. Fix your ball bites on the greens. Go out of your way to repair spike marks if other golfers ahead of your group carelessly failed to tend to them. Happy golf is made up of little things, tiny steps that lead to full appreciation of the game. In real life, it is exactly the same thing. Small steps exercised and completed on a daily basis lead to a fullness of character and an overall sense of well-being.

The honor system goes to the core of golf, as it should with life. Whether or not you should count all your strokes is not even debatable. If you're not honest at golf, you are not even playing the game and should instantly take up a new avocation. Cheating at golf is not only disgraceful behavior to yourself, but it is also a grave disservice and sign of disrespect to the people you cheat. Simply decide early on that you'd rather lose your right arm than cheat at golf. It keeps things really simple and will enhance your peace of mind.

In addition to socializing, the sport of golf also allows you plenty of time to be by yourself. Use this opportunity for silent prayer, quiet reflection. Readjust the rough spots in your life by simply looking around you. Many golf courses are built on a community's most picturesque real estate. Be thankful that you have the chance to breathe the fresh air, absorbing in your vision the colorful kaleidoscope of trees, lakes, rivers, hills, blossoms, birds, clouds, blue sky, sunshine. Treat these elements of nature not as hazards on a golf course but as gifts to be enjoyed. You are very fortunate to be in these surroundings. Appreciate them humbly. You will be filled with peace, serenity, and happiness.

Musings Between Holes

The sentiments just expressed remind me of one of the most puzzling yet most profound of AA's many aphorisms. Many alcoholics in recovery agonize over the short admission that says: "I am a grateful alcoholic." This is a statement of maturity that some attain and many don't. In fact, many folks in AA (or circling around the edges of the commitment that AA requires) kick and scream over this one with the same rage golfers exhibit after flailing away and leaving the ball in a sand trap—three times running. How to be grateful, then?

Let's examine the concept of gratitude, the art of never taking good things or people for granted. Let all the good things we enjoy in America seep over your consciousness, and work to understand that the grasp of gratitude is the art of living well; it is also the key to receiving even more good things so that we can give good things freely. It was Cicero who said, "Gratitude is not only the greatest of virtues, but the parent of all others." Indeed, as generations upon generations have known, gratitude connects us all in the never-ending cycle of life. As President John F. Kennedy was fond of saying: "To whom much is given, much is required."

Forget the game for a bit. Forget what we are trying to accomplish in these pages, weaving as we are between the sport of golf and the art of living. Time for a break. In the macro and the micro views, take time for gratitude. Bear with me for a moment as I remind you of something that, as a golfer, I hope never to take for granted: the absolutely stunning array of golf courses all across this country. From Pine Valley in the East to Augusta in the South, across hundreds of stellar courses in the Midwest, to hundreds more in California, and a handful of my personal favorites in Hawaii, we are truly blessed.

Far from taking up valuable real estate space, these jewels of the sport preserve, respect, celebrate, and enhance the land they occupy. Most of them are public and eminently accessible to anyone, even rank beginners and those who, despite years of practice, still shoot "large." These courses are breathtaking examples of what can happen when sportsmanship and ingenuity collide perfectly with landscape architecture and deep respect for the land.

It's true, besotted with the game as I am, I view courses with a golfer's eyes and still, I can see that many of these courses incorporate the natural beauty of the geography and the surroundings in truly magnificent ways. And even those who aren't in love with or addicted to golf concede that walking a golf course can nurture an appreciation of the outdoors, of horticulture, of nature herself.

Consider Lincoln Park in San Francisco. It was definitely the best place to start for aspiring and soon-to-be-successful golfers with San Francisco roots like Tony Lema, Ken Venturi, Johnny Miller, and John Brodie (a former 49ers quarterback with two-sport credentials as a fierce competitor on the PGA Seniors Tour). And one could do worse than following in the footsteps of Clint Eastwood, currently co-owner of Pebble Beach, the crown jewel of California golf courses.

Lincoln is a workingman golfer's vision of heaven. Shaped to fit the hilly and gracefully flowing bumpiness of the city's ups and downs, this course offers a heart-stopping glimpse of the Pacific Ocean stretching thousands of miles toward Hawaii. Talk about your ultimate water hazard. Perched on the edge of the continent, Lincoln is the very showcase of what draws people to the San Francisco Bay Area. You can catch fleeting moments of the glorious Golden Gate Bridge while setting up your next golf shot. The beauty of it all is life enhancing. Strands of fog play with the bridge's cables like a harpist sent from God. Cargo ships appear to glide beneath tee boxes and greens, creating playful wakes for sailboats and windsurfers. Up on the course, you can hear the barking of harbor seals and California sea lions on the rocks below.

And if your tee shot on a couple of the holes goes a little bit errant, you can retrieve your ball beneath several statues gracing the Legion of Honor, which sits Acropolis-like atop the middle of the golf course. Here, on the grounds of one of San Francisco's most important museums, you might catch sight of Rodin's sculpture *The Thinker*. As you inhale the genius of what may be the artist's best-known work, your soul may well be soothed of the trauma it has suffered from hitting a bad Titleist.

As you wind your way along the cypress-tree-lined edge of the Pacific cliffs, which plunge hundreds of feet down to the surging breaks, you might even stumble into a few historical landmarks while searching for your out-of-bounds tee shot. Weapons bunkers are embedded into the hillside and well camouflaged, first intentionally and now by overgrowth. The bunkers were dug into the earth during the post–Pearl Harbor hysteria that swept the nation and triggered West Coast military forces to prepare for what was feared to be an impending aerial attack by Japanese bomber planes at the height of World War II.

The golf course is traversed several times by the Lincoln Highway, a picturesque route that served as the first road across America. While crossing this road in their golf shoes, golfers can look up at the Holocaust Memorial, easily the most sobering reminder on any golf course anywhere that we should never take any of our freedoms for granted. The open-air exhibit displays lifelike bodies of Holocaust victims sprawled tragically along the ground behind grim chicken-wire fences. Talk about putting one's golf woes in perspective—instantly. Suddenly, the difficulty of your next shot, your entire game, and your work life pale when confronted with this stunningly graphic reminder of the Holocaust and of man's inhumanity to man. This one is tough to beat. This small area, no bigger than a golf green, is just one of the dramatic contrasts that make Lincoln Park so fascinating and so multifaceted. It would take a hardened soul to not feel immense gratitude for all the gifts of life, the gifts of nature, and of pleasures and comforts of golf in this setting. I just pray that the powers that be in San Francisco will invest in bringing this beauty of a course back to her grand splendor.

The Secret

Socrates said that "the unexamined life is not worth living." Examine your life, and the blessings will bubble up. Take the time to reflect, to draw from the pool of wisdom that resides inside your soul. This is your "sacred self," the part of you that's meant to be shared with another. Use your time on the golf course as a tool to deepen the pool of reflection that is the reservoir of your goodness. Let go of your grousing about that last shot or the impossible dogleg coming up. Instead, notice the day and be grateful. Notice where you are and be grateful. Notice the people you're with and be grateful. Remember the ripple effect of your actions, and be grateful that you can have a positive effect on others. And so, the third secret: *Be thoughtful.*

In being thoughtful to your golfing partners, other golfers, the caddies, the greenskeepers, you improve the days—and even the lives—of those around you. Reach down deep and draw from the core of your soul to attain strength and courage, qualities that will add fiber to your life and sweetness to your golf swing. Carry that feeling with you through the game and into your life. Be grateful. Be thoughtful.

With that, I look to *The Cosmic Laws of Golf (and Everything Else):*

> *"The Cosmic Laws of Golf are universal and apply to every activity: golf, work, thinking, talking, mowing the lawn, making art, making love, making money, hauling the garbage, whatever you think, say and do. All wisdom is in the heart of the game and may be used there most fruitfully."*
>
> — Printer Bowler

STEP FIVE

Face the Facts

*N*OW THAT YOU'VE MADE AN INVENTORY OF YOURSELF AND YOUR addiction to golf, what's next? In AA, the next step after that moral inventory is this: *Admitted to God, to ourselves and to another human being the exact nature of our wrongs.*

But think of that in relation to golf. Just as with Step Four, where do you stop? There are so many potential problems with just one swing alone; imagine what the total would be if it included every possibility from even a single game. Never mind a full-blown addiction to the game and all that entails.

Much as I love the game, the inventory of *my* problems with golf could go on forever. Certainly nongolfers would have an entirely different litany: to them, the game appears practically endless, utterly pointless, ridiculously expensive, and an outrageous time sink. I can't deny it. Golf does demand an extraordinary amount of time and attention, attention that might otherwise be directed to profitable pursuits. Or even mowing the lawn. But then the lawn rarely measures up to the green, which gets us back to the clubhouse in a hurry.

So back to that game. The next step?

> *We promised to admit to ourselves and to the other members of our foursome the exact nature of our wrongs on the fairways, sand traps, and greens so that we would be forever free*

*of repeating those dumb-ass mistakes, eternally liberated from
the repetitively stupid thinking that gets us into trouble, and
finally able to gain the sense of happiness and bliss we had hoped
to attain by hitting perfect shots.*

Perfect shots that are all too often completely elusive. Perfect shots that arise from someone else's swing. Certainly not mine. Not today.

Let go, let golf.

Learn from the Tiger: One Shot at a Time

Tiger Woods. Any attempt to analyze his game always comes up short. It's like trying to beat him: usually impossible. But the best explanation for his otherworldly success is his astoundingly ferocious devotion and focus to each shot.

He possesses both the ability to let go of each previous shot—be it good or bad—and the rare talent of focusing utterly, completely, and unconditionally on the next shot. It's as if his universe shrinks to one moment at a time, with no backsplash, no overflow. It's the accumulation of these separate masterpieces that gives shape and substance to his golfing genius.

And then there are the rest of us. One of the best-known and most deeply feared mysteries of golf is how the first tee shot of the day can make or break a golfer. It has all the makings of a superstition. It's completely irrational, of course. Even playing only nine holes, any player will have ample time to recover from an errant first swing. But time and time again, evidence shows that golfers simply plummet into a deep groove of self-loathing and despair following an initial mistake. The pattern dooms them. The Golf Gods seize upon this weakness and haunt the self-pitying golfer the rest of the day.

Not Tiger. Somehow, Tiger Woods possesses an innate, crazily strong ability to defy this doomsday sense of inevitability. He may cuss, rant, and rave following a bad shot, but he also immediately reaches into his soul, steadies himself, remembers who he is and what he is about, and comes up with a recovery that makes the previously evil ball a short and very bad memory. He certainly appears to simply let go, let golf. In an instant. And *he's* playing for enormous stakes.

Stakes or no, reaching into your soul offers you the same assortment of choices that reaching into your golf bag affords. Take a breath. Let hope spring eternal. There is always a better solution to a temporary lapse in judgment. For Tiger, a bad shot is always a severe aberration, never a pattern. That's a mindset to emulate.

In contrast, we all know someone who is the exact opposite of Tiger. Not just in his score but in his very being and approach to the game. It seems there's someone (and consider it good luck if there's *only* one) on every course who plays an entirely different game. Someone who bemoans practically every shot. Someone who completely ignores every basic rule of golf etiquette. Someone who takes it a step further and seems to believe that the niceties of the game may apply to others but certainly not to him or to his game. Who thinks it's all about *his* game, *his* score. Why shouldn't he take his shot as soon as he gets to his ball? Why should he wait for someone else? This is someone who is completely score driven. So much so that he'll forget a few strokes—and with some regularity. He'll take a mulligan any chance he gets. He's proficient at slyly bumping a ball back onto the fairway. He does nothing but complain about bad shots. Sometimes while throwing a club.

What is that? The tantrums of a two-year-old toddler on a golf course? Get a life. Get that ego in check. And keep it there, or you won't stand a chance of breaking 100 and certainly never 90. In case you're wondering, yes, I imagine there are female golfers who fall into this category of golfers—golfers who are so rude and uncontrolled you don't want to be on the course with them, and certainly not in their foursome—but, I'll confess, the examples who spring to my mind are male. Not men, as in adult and reasoned, but male.

The thing is, in addition to annoying everyone around them, the temper tantrums that these people demonstrate do them absolutely no good. Quite the opposite, in fact. Over time, they'll lose their golfing partners. And if they started out playing with their work or life partners, they may lose them as well. Who wants to be around those dark clouds? Who wants what might be called a Golfer from Hell in their foursome, or even in the foursome in front or behind? And what makes them think they've got a right to complain about their shots? Rather than being "legends in their own minds" (as they are often referred to in private), these are people to be avoided—at least until they grow up.

Stepping Up to Play

Back when I was slowly graduating from lessons and practice to actual play, I knew few people who were willing to include a new-to-the-game golfer. So it is with much fondness that I remember the first foursome I was invited into. My dear friends Joe and Debbie Schell are a remarkable couple. The love and affection they feel for each other is visible to all. While that alone shouldn't be particularly remarkable, it is—especially since they also golf together. They are all too rare: a couple who can readily demonstrate their support for each other, even on the golf course. As anyone who has golfed knows, the underbelly of a marriage is often exposed on the course. Too many bad shots, too much advice, even a squeaky wheel on the golf cart, and it's all over. Not so Debbie and Joe. Aside from being good golfers, they play with great respect for each other and with obvious enjoyment.

So I was thrilled to be included in a Schell foursome. Debbie knew I was coming up short on playing partners and invited me to play with her—and two other women. I had a wonderful time and found that I learned a lot about golf and about the social side of the game. Later, as I started to play in more and more all-male foursomes (sometimes with one of the aforementioned "legends") I realized what a gift Debbie's offer (and repeated inclusion in her group) had been. In fact, although I'm careful where I say it, I do think men could learn a lot by playing golf with women. *Playing*, and not feeling the need to power through. *Playing*, not trying to dominate the game, but to play it as it needs to be played. With finesse and calm. Play long enough, and you'll learn (as these women taught me, very quickly) that slamming the ball because you're upset at the last shot simply doesn't work, no matter where you tee up.

Musings Between Holes

When I'm at risk of falling into the trap of fuming over mistakes (on the course and elsewhere), I remember how thoroughly and completely Master Vin defused my anger, long, long ago. I was sputtering and venting about something one of the higher-ups in the military chain of command had done. It was, to my mind, utterly outrageous. Unforgivable, even. And while Master Vin appeared to listen, he just smiled. The more he smiled, the more worked up I got. A little part of me must have thought he just didn't hear what I was saying. Maybe I was hoping he'd really pay attention to me if I stormed enough. Instead, before I got wound up for a second crescendo, he quietly asked if he could share a story with me.

And off he went, on a long elaborate story of two monks. Two monks? I was upset about the military, and he wanted to talk about monks? But Master Vin continued, explaining that the monks were walking the long miles back to their monastery. They walked through a village, then past the village. Then they came to a stream that was rushing higher and faster than they'd ever seen it. And there, beside the stream, sat a pregnant woman. She needed to get back to her village, on the other side, but was worried that she'd lose her footing and get swept away. Master Tinh asked her permission to help, calmly picked her up, and carried her across the stream. Master Quan followed along, a dignified distance behind. As soon as they were across, Master Tinh carefully set the woman down and bid her farewell as she turned and headed off toward her village. The two monks continued on toward the monastery in silence. Miles passed under their feet. Finally, as the monastery came into sight, Master Quan broke his silence, expressing his shock at what the other monk had done. He had picked up a woman! How could he have done such a thing? It was clear by his tone that he was horrified.

Master Tinh replied, with utter calm and perfect serenity: "I carried her for but a moment; you have carried her for all these miles and all these hours."

Hard to argue that one. I do have to relearn it from time to time, but what a lesson and what a reminder. Talk about letting it go! Let it go, and move on.

The Secret

You can't change what's happened. But you can learn. And it's how you respond to what happens in your life—good, bad, and mediocre—that really defines the outcome. Nothing stays the same. Not even one hole on a golf course is exactly the same as it was the last time you played it. Not the grass, not the wind, especially not the sand traps. So too, life is a process of one challenge after another. Nobody gets through unscathed. So here's the secret: *Learn from the speed bumps.*

Yes, sometimes if you're careful, you can drive around the speed bumps or at least slow down for them so you don't lose control. But sometimes you don't see them in advance; sometimes (some would say always) they're there for a reason. Discard the notion that stress can be eliminated or medicated away. Instead, teach yourself to think of stress and challenges as opportunities, not emotional crises. Learn to do this on the golf course and think how much better your game may become. Did you find yourself flailing, stuck in a sand trap? Don't stick your head in the sand and pretend you will never land there again. Instead, spend an afternoon practicing your chip shot, so the next time you're sure to get out in one stroke, well placed.

Successful people thrive on challenges. Most of them will tell you that they have learned more from their failures than they ever did from their successes. Far from being intimidated by speed bumps, they learned to study them, accept them, and gently glide past them onto their next accomplishment—on the course and in life. Witness Tiger and his attitude:

> *"I realize that a poor shot is just a swing away. I also realize that once I've hit a poor shot my only recourse is to hit a better shot on the next swing. In other words, I've learned how to hit it and forget it. There's no sense dwelling on a mistake. You can't hit the shot again, so forget about it."*
>
> — Tiger Woods

STEP SIX

Be Ready, for It All Counts

*A*DMITTING TO WRONGS IS ONE THING; DOING SOMETHING ABOUT THEM is entirely different. It's enough to make some addicts wish they'd never even considered Step Five. But, like many of AA's precepts, it's one step at a time, and this time it's: *Were entirely ready to have God remove all these defects of character.*

Nice, isn't it, to think that God could fix our golf game? But, really, it's hard (at least for some of us) to imagine that golf is anywhere on God's radar. Certainly there are bigger problems in this world than golf. So let's look to those lesser beings, the Golf Gods, and see what they can (or might) do (if they so choose).

> *We decided that, by invoking the Golf Gods, by pleading for their help, we might get their help in exorcising the devious yips, shakes, and storms of self-doubt that haunt us during our game. And then, finally, with the help of the Golf Gods, our inner pro could take over, kick in, and put our minds and bodies and souls on automatic pilot—and release that perfect game.*

You've had the lessons; you've watched the pros. *Endlessly.* Some part of you knows what to do, but those other parts and those golfing glitches just keep getting in the way. Maybe it *is* time for the automatic pilot. Could it be any worse than that pathetic round you had (how long ago?) that's still rattling around in your head?

Let go, let golf.

The Yips Are to Golf
What High Anxiety Is to Life

Yips? Another golf term. According to wiseGEEK's informative website, former professional golfer Tommy Armour is "credited with inventing the term *yips* to describe a combination of psychological and neuromuscular factors that forced his early retirement from competitive golf." What are the yips? They are described as "involuntary twitches of the hands or lower arms that cause golfers to shank simple putts." Occurring as they often do, right as the club head meets the ball, they can ruin a putt in a hurry. Armour is not alone; many veteran golfers struggle with the yips, most often in short putting situations under pressure. Some players experience them in other shots as well. Is it just pressure?

It would seem there is no definitive answer as to what causes yips, but the theories fall into two main camps. Some believe that the yips are triggered by the psychological pressures surrounding an important golf shot, such as a game-winning putt. Certainly those are the yips that get the most attention, the most screen time, and the most press. It makes sense that (despite all the best training), the intensity of an audience, a cash incentive, and the adrenaline rush of competition can cause a golfer to lose focus during a putt. This theory has support in the number of professional golfers who demonstrate the yips when the stakes are very high.

But even the sports psychologists and experts in sports medicine aren't sure. It could be that the yips are primarily neuromuscular. Could be they're simple muscle spasms due to golfers' tendency to assume awkward putting positions for extended periods of time. And the yips aren't exclusive to golfers. Yips exist in other sports, and even dentists, surgeons, and musicians exhibit them. The common threads? Intricate hand and lower arm coordination—and pressure. Whether it's the pressure to make a perfect shot (with a golf ball or a basketball) or a perfect throw (basketball or baseball), perform delicate surgery, or complete awkward fingering on a musical instrument, a yip can be a nightmare for a lot of people. A recurring yip? Even worse.

Bert Yancey, a professional golfer in the late 1960s and early 1970s, was much admired by professionals and fans alike. He was known for the fluid grace of his drives and the precision of his putts. But, after some years of erratic behavior, he was finally diagnosed with manic depression in the 1970s. Treatment with lithium controlled his disease (now commonly called bipolar disorder) but resulted in hand tremors that all but destroyed his once-flawless game. Despite the tremors, he became an acclaimed teaching pro, but needed an assistant to demonstrate the strokes. In 1984, he was switched to Tegretol, a medication that caused less-pronounced side effects. Yancey was able to resume tournament play in 1987 and joined the Seniors Tour when he turned fifty in 1988. To many, his return to professional golf seemed nothing short of miraculous, even though he did not regain his old mastery. But for Yancey, who lectured widely on his disease over the years, even playing golf poorly was a relief. As he put it in 1987, when he finished fifty-second in his first tournament since 1976, "I've been in padded cells and straitjackets, and, believe me, this is better."

Yancey died of a heart attack on August 26, 1994. According to *Golf Central*, this occurred moments before he was due on the tee at the Franklin Quest Championship at Park Meadows Golf Club in Park City, Utah. An inscription at the club, dedicated to Yancey, reads: "Bert Yancey was a tenacious champion with unusual courage, determination, wit and wisdom. As a true professional, he exemplified persistence through hardship. He had an undying passion for preserving the history and integrity of golf. His quest for excellence remained remarkably intense and focused as he executed his final shot from this area."

Puts the little yips the rest of us might experience from time to time in perspective, doesn't it? Time then to focus on some of the other missteps we make when under stress, glitches that are larger than yips, and much more significant.

Be Glad It's Not You

Remember that composite Golfer from Hell, in the last chapter? I've encountered more than a few of them—and (especially given my age) I've not been golfing long. Could be that if you've been golfing since you were a child, it's possible to just shake your head, let their misbehavior roll off of you, and move on. I haven't reached that point; instead, I find myself wondering, what got them there? And, just as importantly, what *keeps* them there? And I don't mean on the golf course but in that foul state of gloom and self-centeredness that pushes everyone else away. Never mind what it does to their golf game—and sometimes to the golf game and energy of everyone unfortunate enough to cross their paths.

Could be a side effect of what I've done in my professional life, but I wonder: What old wounds are they harboring? Were they not loved as children? Are they not loved as adults? Why are they so armored? So self-centered? Is there abuse or even addiction buried in there? Or did they simply learn bad habits from another Golfer from Hell? And, having taken on those habits, can't they look outside of themselves far enough to see how other people enjoy the game, the day, and each other? Much as I like to think of golf as therapeutic, clearly it's not so for everyone, and maybe it's just the wrong therapy for some.

If it's a friend who's suddenly exhibiting Golfer from Hell behavior, I'll initiate a conversation to try to help. Often enough, that's all the opening someone needs to talk about a difficulty and move past it. But always the specter of Golfer from Hell behavior serves as a reminder and a warning to me. It's simple, but true: what you put out there is what you get. And if you have children or work with them in any way, know that everything is seen and absorbed—everything.

Everything Counts

Everything counts—and I don't mean simply all of your strokes. (No question: you must count them all, every single one.) *Everything counts* is much bigger than that. If you saw Jack Nicholson's speech at the 1998 Golden Globe Awards ceremony, this phrase may well have stuck with you. Nicholson had just been awarded best performance by an actor for his role in the brilliantly written and scripted James Brooks film *As Good as It Gets.* The reliably irreverent Nicholson can always be counted on to elicit roars of adulation and yelps of praise from his adoring peers and fans. But on this night Nicholson took the stage with beads of sweat on his brow and a quaking vocal twitch in his pipes.

Perhaps it was the somewhat poignant and compelling subject matter of the film, in which a previously homophobic writer (played by Nicholson) in the latter stages of his career befriends a neighbor and conquers his fears. Or perhaps it was because the legendarily anarchistic actor is surprisingly shy and emotional in small gatherings. Whatever the circumstances, Nicholson chose to champion the hard work and unsung heroics of movie people behind the scenes—the underpaid understudies, the technical crew, the makeup people, the caterers, all the support people—and all the countless deeds performed by countless bit players in an extravaganza that ultimately spotlights only one or two superstars.

In a charming moment of disarming humility, Nicholson discarded his prepared notes and looked into the camera with unscripted sincerity. With a trembling wave of emotion in his voice, he then blurted out: "What I am trying to tell you is that everything counts." Underscoring the moment with his trademark flatness of tone, he repeated, "Every little thing . . . *counts.*"

It was a gallant and heartfelt expression of deep gratitude, one that provided a profound insight into what the film business is all about—a celebration of collegiality and mutual respect. In an instant, one realized with sudden immediacy the full range of the famous actor's good fortunes. Not the financial gains so much as the bliss and happiness that comes from providing a service which is the product of passionate teamwork, uncompromising dedication, deep respect for minor deeds usually overlooked, and communal trust in the people with whom he works.

Wow. It was a completely revealing few minutes of self-examination. *Everything counts.* Let that sink in.

On the golf course, it is a vital principle to absorb. Not only does every stroke count—literally and figuratively—but every thought, every action, every word, every feeling, as well. It's a simple thing to tell yourself to keep a positive attitude and go out there and shoot the lights out. It's quite another to perform.

Walk yourself through a mood swing. Try to understand how quickly the tide can change, and, more importantly, learn to accept and shape those swings to your advantage. We all know first-tee euphoria. You've made it through a tough week, and now it's time to play. The sky is a sparkling blue, the dewy smell of fresh-cut grass fills your lungs with new life, your friends are happy and chatty. You are staring at a brand-new Titleist Pro V1 perched on your tee waiting to fly down the middle of the first fairway. Suddenly, life becomes a beer commercial. It doesn't get any better than this.

Then, in one devious swoop of the sport's treacherous betrayal, your "feel" abandons you, and your first drive is a pathetic 150-yard blooper off to the right. You feel the blood rush to your face. You tell yourself that, deep down, you are no good. In that instant, a cloud appears in the sky and hovers over your heart. Instead of that delicious moment you were enjoying mere seconds ago, you have catapulted into the downward spiral of losers, whiners, underachievers, and the depressed (and depressing) purveyors of mediocrity.

Why do we do this to ourselves? Why do we allow this to happen? It is, indeed, a mystery, both in life and golf. But if you truly grasp the meaning of *everything counts*, you will come to realize that this is *only* one bad shot in a daylong experience. It's no omen. Let it go. Learn from it. Everything counts. Everything is valuable. Gain the balance. Thrive on both mistake and success. I truly think this is one of the most important keys to maintaining a solid, healthy attitude as we stride the fairways of our lives and the roughs of our golf courses.

Life can be incredibly tedious, humdrum, devoid of thrills. But those who see the value in all the little, common things will accrue wisdom and strength from paying attention to them and using them as stepping stones to success. It starts with making your bed in the morning. Don't laugh. That's life's first tee. Even when you don't feel like doing it, just do it. Something changes. A page has been turned. A new day has begun well. That's a good definition of how to attain a fresh new attitude. Nothing comes to us without effort, but when we take the first step, the dynamics click into motion.

Everything counts. On the golf course, embrace it all. The "feel" comes and goes. We'd love to have it all day long, but, to my knowledge, nobody in the history of the sport has ever shot eighteen eagles in one round. Everything counts. How you greet the starter in the golf course. How you treat your friends on the links. What you tell yourself in those long moments of silence and solitude. What you choose to acquire from the spirit of the competition, things you will bring to the rest of your life as sustaining enhancement.

Everything counts. Good feelings, bad shots, moments of clarity, long periods of confusion and doubt, brief moments of ecstasy, bouts with frustration and anger, expressions of admiration and praise. Embrace it all. And always remember, the greatest glory comes not from avoiding falls, but in learning how to rise again every time we do fall.

Musings Between Holes

As you're walking between holes, pondering the importance of *everything counts*, think of this: children are universally inclined to emulate the behavior of the people they see around them. It's why there's much truth in the adage

"The apple doesn't fall far from the tree." And in the long run, it's modeling the behavior you want to see that counts the most.

So keep that *everything counts* thought in mind as you're walking the golf course and beyond. Golf may be just a game, but it is part of your life. And, depending upon how much you golf, it's a not inconsiderable amount of time in your life. When you're out in nature, enjoying the day, why not aim to make your behavior on the golf course as sublime as the natural layout? If you've got devilish sand traps of your own, leave them behind. The traps on the course are more than enough to deal with.

The Secret

Even if you're playing a practice round by yourself, why not be kind to yourself? Shush that grumbling voice, and notice the good shots. Enjoy the game. Yes, you may want to work on a shot or two, but be the kindest possible teacher. Not only will you have a better time, you'll be in the habit for the next time you're with your favorite foursome. Whether you have children in your foursome or friends who are your contemporaries, know that you do have an influence. Not just on the mood of the group and the flavor of the day, but on what everyone carries home with them. And even what attitude others take out onto the course for the next round.

The reality is that advising others to "Do what I say to do" simply doesn't work. The golf pro can say that forever, but until you watch his magnificent stroke, hear the steps broken down (maybe even repeatedly), and really, really practice it, you'll keep on doing what you've been doing. That troublesome stroke you're trying to purge will stick with you, no matter how wrong it is and no matter how much it doesn't work for your game. It takes work. And you've got to see the right stroke—a lot.

We all learn by example, so just as the golf pro, do your best to make your example a good one. The secret? *Take responsibility for your actions: everything—every little thing—counts.*

Everything counts. And everything is connected. We all—children, teens, adults, golfers, even those mysterious nongolfers—should understand that how we *behave* today plants all the seeds for the future, ours and others'. It's just the law of life. It's that simple. Take that first step, follow it with more, and good things can begin to happen. But if that first step is in the wrong direction, look out—and turn around before you're in the wrong place, and have pulled others with you. An example? If, in a weak moment, a kid cheats in school (maybe she's seen you cheat on the golf course?), would her friends want to do business with her in the future? All your actions, even the smallest ones, have consequences for you or for those who follow in your footsteps. Make bad choices today, and you may end up hurt, seriously and permanently injured, dead, or in jail. Why not use your energy on making good choices, healthy ones that will have direct, specific, and positive outcomes later in life? Why not build the right habits on the golf course and with every step? As you're making yours a great game, ponder this, from *Golf's Greatest Moments*:

> *"Golf is the most individual of sports. We can compete against our playing partners on the course, but ultimately we are playing against ourselves. This aspect of golf makes it both intensely exhilarating and exasperating, and because golf is such an individual sport, it tends to magnify our personal character strengths and flaws."*

> — Robert Sidorsky

STEP SEVEN

Drop the Shortcomings and Aim for Serenity

S O NOW, AFTER STEP SIX IN THE AA LIST, WE'RE READY TO HAVE DEFECTS of character removed. AA's Step Seven? *Humbly asked Him to remove our shortcomings.*

Asking is one thing. But actually removing those shortcomings is a pretty tall order. Well, maybe not so tall an order for God, but still, it seems like a lot from this angle. We've all got our share of shortcomings—and, on bad days, what seem like more than our share. (At least I know *I* do, and I assume I'm not alone in this.) And we've all got shortcomings in our lives and in how we lead our lives.

After a particularly rough day on the links, we may feel unspeakably long on shortcomings, golf-related and otherwise. And yet we have read every book, subscribed to every golf magazine, tried every "fool-proof" method. Foolproof or not, still we feel foolish, *and* still we don't execute on the golf course. Some days, it seems that shortcomings are *all* we've got. On those days, if we remove our shortcomings in golf, we can't even make it around the course. So what then? Then we bargain.

> *Okay, Golf Gods. We know that golf, like life, simply is not fair. We know we'll never be perfect, that we can only set perfection as a goal, and be understanding with ourselves when we fall*

51

short (or long, or completely miss the green). What about if on our good days, when we're playing decently, what about if then you remove our shortcomings—just the shortcomings in our golf game? And if that's too much, how about you just let us have one decent shot?

Let go, let golf.

Serenity and Intensity

I cannot think of two words that better encapsulate what we are trying to accomplish here than *serenity* and *intensity*. To play golf well, to live life well, demands both.

Need an example of serenity and intensity in action on the golf course? Picture Tiger Woods. No, not in a meltdown. Picture him in his more normal mode in tournament play. When he is focused and drilled in, which happens on just about every stroke, there comes over his face a very specific look of ferocious engagement—and a gaze of detached wonderment. Serene, intense. That just about says it all.

I truly believe that this state of combined serenity and intensity can be attained through hard work. Most of us have no idea what kinds of incredible things can happen once we decide to get ourselves out of the way of . . . ourselves. As disciplined practitioners of yoga can attest: "When the pupil is ready, the teacher appears." What makes the pupil ready can be any number of things, most of them indefinable. But one constant is that this level of awareness is rarely accomplished without intense effort and long hours of work.

In Search of the Aha!
From Confusion to Effort to Clarity

One friend uses his experience in the study of a foreign language—Latin, in his case—to illustrate the Aha! moment of sudden clarity. Back when he was a freshman in high school and struggling mightily to grasp this strange new world of foreign tongues and obscure vocabulary, Latin seemed formidable. As if there weren't enough of life's other distractions besieging him (remember peer pressure, adolescence, dating, family problems, and puberty?), now came the baffling world of Latin and all its declensions. He failed test after test, but never gave up trying. He read the words aloud at night, and applied himself to all the tedious exercises that made about as much sense to him as advanced calculus. He carried flip cards in his back pocket and referred to them many times during the day.

Then, one morning during Latin class, he had an experience that was like scales falling from his eyes. For him, it was like staring forever at one of those artistic optical illusions in which the foreground and background switch. Others could immediately see the vase transform into the candlesticks or the young, proper Victorian lady morph into the old crone. But for him, the longer he stared, the more obscure became the picture. Finally, with Latin, enough blinking and thinking produced results. He started to fully grasp the meaning of all things Latin and suddenly saw how the etymology explained much of English. Instead of resigning to the challenge as some cruel high school hazing, he hung in there, refused to quit, and was finally rewarded with solution of the puzzle.

He does not pretend to understand the exact dynamics of the process, but he does know that he never would have "gotten it" had he abandoned his efforts anywhere along the line. Today, he is an avid wordsmith who expresses himself articulately in English. Beyond that, he understands the precise historical and cultural essence of the words he so carefully chooses in conversations both formal and casual. He never gave up. He won the prize.

It's the same, isn't it, when you think about where you are with your golfing ability? You spent hours reading the books and magazines. You spent countless hours past dusk on the driving range. You studied your heroes on TV. When you could afford golf lessons, you signed up. When you couldn't, you listened with increased care as TV commentators analyzed swing after swing. You were barraged with information and various opinions, but you kept applying yourself. Finally, over time, you learned to relax with your God-given swing, and you learned to become comfortable with the motions that best suited your personal body mechanics. You didn't abandon all those hard-earned sources of information. Quite the contrary. You eased them into your consciousness, and they became threads in the fabric of your understanding. Those hard-earned gains are now in a relaxed state ready to be accessed. Intensity leads to serenity. You start to swing the club happily, with abandon and a sense of relaxation and overall well-being. Good things are happening. You are, at last, "getting it." Intensity and serenity. Let go. Let golf.

There's a reason I keep coming back to those words, *serenity* and *intensity*. Nothing better explains the underlying theme of this book. After hard work and long preparation—sometimes in desperate hours when you have no idea what you are doing or when the results will appear—a very profound value called trust begins to reveal itself. You are tasting what it is to trust your life, to trust your golf shot. There is no price tag for the value of trust. It is simply the key to a life well lived, a sport expertly played. Trust and confidence are the triggers that allow your God-given abilities to flow and shine.

The Opposite of Aha!

But wait. For all that serenity and intensity, even Tiger stumbles. Rarely, literally. Remember, he played the 2008 U.S. Open months after surgery on his left knee, sometimes limping, once using two clubs as canes to get out of a bunker. On the last of ninety holes, he came up to tie Rocco Mediate—and then won on the first hole of a sudden death. Afterward, Tiger conducted interviews, calmly and with grace. It was not until days later that we learned he had played with a double stress fracture of his left tibia. Truly amazing fortitude and grace.

But sometimes he does let a few words slip. Yep, he is human.

Some players know how to keep their cussing to a bare, rare minimum. Others may flare up quickly over a bad shot, then right away laugh at themselves and apologize to others for their behavior. I suspect most of us are in this latter category. And then there's a third category: players who simply can't believe that every shot they make is not perfect, players I've referred to earlier as Golfers from Hell. You've seen them on the golf course. Red-faced, pouting, moping, throwing clubs, hurling epithets, these people simply cannot accept or handle the imperfection of their game. Not surprisingly, when they *do* make a good shot, their outward displays of self-congratulation border on the narcissistic. Extreme cases, yes, but every one of them is a handful.

Tommy Bolt, a colorful golfer in the 1950s, was a case in point. Bolt was a member of the 1955 and 1957 U.S. Ryder Cup teams. An eighteen-time champion on both the regular and senior PGA tours (including winning the U.S. Open title in 1958), Bolt was inducted into the World Golf Hall of Fame in 2002. Despite all these accolades, however, he may be best known for the tempestuous bouts of rage that he displayed with full fury on the golf course.

A story is told, in various forms, reflecting Bolt's off-the-scale temper. As one version goes, toward the end of one of his infamous high-volume, temperamental, club-throwing rounds, "Terrible Tommy" asked his caddie for a club recommendation for a shot of about 155 yards. His caddie responded, "I'd say either a 3-iron or a wedge, sir." Bolt blasted back, "3-iron or a wedge? What kind of stupid choice is that?" As graciously as possible under the circumstances, the caddie gave his honest reply: "Those are the only two clubs you have left, sir."

True or not, legends such as these grew up for good reason around Bolt (variously referred to as "Thunder," "Terrible," or "Tempestuous") in his day. Now, much as I am a staunch believer in the separation of church and golf, I have always been amused by temper tantrums in fellow golfers. And, frankly, I don't think most of us are good enough to complain anyway, and since doing so gets in the way of the next "better shot," why not just let go! In fact, why not do it one better?

Instead of Cussing, How About Quick Silent Prayers?

This is no theology book, but I will say there are a few things I do on the golf course that consistently serve me well. Because I believe that we learn more from our failures than we do from our successes, I am actually grateful for both. And when I find myself in a crisis (whether a true crisis or just a crisis) I remind myself that the Chinese character, or ideogram, for crisis includes a brush stroke for danger and another for opportunity. When I make a terrific shot beyond my usual stable of tricks, I smile inwardly and utter a thought of thanks. I do the same when I make a bad shot. A bad shot? I know that analyzing the bad shot will open up more information for me to absorb. It's a satisfying balancing act that gives me an inner smile for realizing it all fits together.

There's plenty to be grateful for when you are walking around a golf course. The freedom to play, the joy that comes from being with good friends, the weather and sunshine that make you feel healthy and wholesome—these are things we should never take for granted. The good shots are extra bonuses— whenever they occur. And accepting both good and bad shots is a perfect model to emulate when living our daily lives. What doesn't destroy us makes us strong, as Nietzsche so sagely advised us.

Good things come from these internal conversations. My golf game stays on an even keel, my blood pressure stays under par, and the behavior I practice on the golf course spills over into my daily life in positive ways that serve to improve my relationships with others. It's a great way to achieve a certain level of serenity in a game that's full of stress and in a life that's packed with high levels of expectation. Really. There's enough stress in life. Why carry that onto the golf course?

High Hopes

Bob Hope certainly packed a lot in. Between his movies, television shows, and travels to entertain troops around the world, he pushed himself over a very long career. And always he loved his golf. He also knew how to enjoy and savor every moment, as this poignant story makes clear. In late 2002, mere months before his death, the famed actor and comedian was traveling around the San Francisco Bay Area in a limousine with his wife, Dolores. Knowing he did not have much longer to live, Hope was taking in his favorite scenery of the Bay Area. There's plenty of scenery to enjoy, and it seems Hope had something specific in mind. After winding through the countryside on the far end of Sir Francis Drake Boulevard, the limousine came to a crawl on the roadway that dissects the San Geronimo Golf Course. The chauffeur pulled to the shoulder, emerged from the vehicle, and opened the back door. Out stepped Hope—comedian, crooner, and golfer—with his trademark golf club. Walking toward the second tee with his familiar jaunty pace slowed only slightly by age, Hope belted a few balls down the middle of the fairway, then turned on his heel and strode back to the waiting limo. Hope folded himself in, the chauffeur got back behind the wheel, and the limo took off toward the Pacific horizon and the rest of Bob Hope's life. He said it best, and often: Thanks for the memory.

Musings Between Holes

Readers of certain age will be humming a Bob Hope tune right now. But everyone knows just how important memories are. And how important it is to connect with generations other than our own. We can all learn by playing with and listening to people outside our age group. Even way outside.

As I practice gratitude about golf—about the opportunities I have to play, not necessarily *how* I play—I try to remember to approach golf not only as recreation but also as a viable and positive agent of change working wonders in people's lives. At one particular course, I see that happening all the time.

It's the Mill Valley Golf Club, a landscaper's marvel situated in the middle of a small town in southern Marin and an excellent "starter" course for kids and older novices taking up the game for the first time. Very short in yardage and only nine holes long, this little demon tests every bit of your patience and skill. Nested beneath Mount Tamalpais, the course has creeks and steep hillsides that challenge golfers normally used to sprawling fairways unimpeded by ancient trees and irksome rivulets. Tees are constructed on horrible mats (like the kind you used to see on driving ranges of old—not unlike a really bad doormat) that play havoc with the rhythm of your swing and the integrity of your equipment. For all its natural beauty, this course tests players' patience and skill. In short, the course wins, and, all too often, players lose their tempers. But not a certain group of players.

Some days, the best part of this hellish little course is the opportunity to meet the old-timers, some of whom might appear to have been playing since the club's inception in 1919. These golfers have lived full lives, they are eager to share, and they have a wealth of insights—about the course, about golf, and about life. The stories they can tell, not only about the sport that drives (the rest of) us nuts but also about the local history of the surrounding area, are stories to hear and to heed. And it's here (and on courses like it) that one of golf's most valuable benefits takes hold. We have the chance to socialize with and learn from others and to build new friendships. The course is only nine holes. You can take your time to enjoy it and enjoy all the stories. Hurry through, and you miss a lot. Why not learn to savor the moment? Why not learn to listen?

It's not a new thought, but listening really does matter. And there's a lot to listen to on the golf course. Between the sounds of nature, the conversations, the thwack of the ball, it's quite a concert. And it's all in what you listen to, and when. One of the most noticeable leaps in my game came as a direct result of my listening to someone I'd just met.

I was treating myself to the luxury of an extra day near Pinehurst, North Carolina. I'd been nearby for a board meeting and just couldn't resist the call of that fabulous golf course. But I was by myself, not always the easiest situation where you're not a member and not local. Add to that the fact that I was then very new to golf, pretty much freshly minted. Burt, the caddy who took me on, was older than I and well versed in the course and the entire game. We talked a bit as I warmed up on the practice tee. The usual stuff, but I realized he was assessing my stroke very thoroughly.

In no time, I found myself added in with a man and his teenage son as they were just teeing up—back at the tips. The tips? So much for the sigh of relief I'd breathed when I first saw the son, and assumed he was a beginner. Young and plenty strong, but still a beginner, like me. Or so I thought, until the dad asked if I'd play the tips with them. Before I could mumble that I was "sort of a beginner," Burt stopped me with a look. He then strode closer and murmured to me, "You'll do fine from the tips. Just hit like you're on the driving range."

With that vote of confidence (based on what: a few decent swings and drives?) Burt did more for my game than a whole series of lessons might have. He bolstered my trust in my swing and in my game. And, yes, he gave me more than a few hints about the course along the way. Enough hints that between his guidance and my newly relaxed game, I was ahead at the turn and at the end of the round. For my first time on the tips, that was quite an accomplishment—and a serious testament to the benefit of having someone older (especially a caddy) exhibit confidence in you.

The Secret

Happily, I have nothing but the fondest memories of Pinehurst. But that might not have been the case. Had it not been for my luck in having Burt as a caddy—and listening to him—chances are I'd have blown that entire round of golf. I'd have undermined what skills I had by worrying about performing. Not unusual. We really are our own worst enemies, in both life and sport. But with the right words from a mentor, with a boost when we need it, success is easier. The secret? *Let it go. Let it go and get out of your own way.*

It's time for all of us to take a huge breath, don't you think? Bring back the simple enjoyments that too much success has spoiled and too much failure has soured. We should live and play somewhere in the middle of those extremes. What happened to laughing at ourselves? Where did humility go to hide? When did we choose to boast too much about agility and mope too much about fragility? When are we ever going to get out of the way of ourselves? In this season of my life I say a daily prayer to stay out my own way. I can tell you with all my heart it really does allow for good things to flow.

> *"The cliché about the game being you against the golf course is only partly true. Ultimately, it is you against yourself. It always comes down to how well you know yourself, your ability, your limitations and the confidence you have in your ability to execute under pressure that is mostly self-created. Ultimately, you must have the heart and head to play a shot and the courage to accept the consequences."*

> — Tiger Woods

STEP EIGHT

Golf as a Gift

𝓔 VEN IF WE'RE SUDDENLY PURGED OF OUR OWN PERSONAL SHORTCOM-
ings, they've been around a long time. And over the years they've had
their own ripple effects, most likely not positive ones. AA's next step recognizes this. Step Eight? *Made a list of all persons we had harmed, and became
willing to make amends to them all.*

All persons we had harmed? I always yell "fore," I haven't beaned anyone (at
least yet) and besides, some days I hit the ball so poorly, if it made contact,
it wouldn't hurt. If anyone has picked up bad habits by watching my golf
swing, am I accountable for that? Isn't that their fault? But wait: let's not be
literal here. What if . . .

> *As part of our plea to the Golf Gods, we express a willingness to
> make a list of all the people hurt by our abuse of golf—spouses
> spending the day alone, employers who thought we were tak-
> ing a sick day (when we were simply sick of not getting enough
> golf), kids waiting sadly in the driveway with baseball gear. And
> it doesn't stop at nongolfers. What about the fellow golfers—and
> our better selves—we thought we had fooled by posting false
> scores? We do need to be willing to make amends—somehow,
> some way—to all those we have harmed.*

Let go, let golf.

Tempering Effects

As far as I know, very few people have ever been hit with a golf club. At least not intentionally. But what about all those words that are flung around? Those tirades out on the course—muttered, screamed, or something in between—do have immediate and ripple effects. It doesn't take a Tommy Bolt to make other players uncomfortable. Or to drive away their concentration with a few loud profanities, punctuating the game. Or even to make another player pick up the habit of a bad temper.

You may well be playing with a salty old crew for whom even the most creatively constructed curse is nothing new. But know that you and your foursome are not the only ones out there. Not by a long shot. Sounds (and the visuals) do carry across a course. And across the clubhouse. Is that how you want to be known? To teenagers experimenting with social networking sites online, we advise to never put up anything you wouldn't want your grandmother to see. The same concept applies at the golf course—to your mouth and to your behavior. And it's not just that you might wind up on a website of golfers gone amok (those sites *do* exist) but that your behavior may be adopted by someone else coming behind you (literally or figuratively). Remember, as emphasized back in Step Six, everything counts. So instead of just charging on ahead, as usual, think about your actions. Not just your golf form; your actions. Start practicing your behavior so it's what you'd like your grandchildren to see or hear about, now or in family stories later. That means not giving in to the dark side of golfing. No tirades, no cheating, not even any grumbling. What on earth could have caused that grumbling, anyway? If you've done your own imitation of Terrible Tommy over the years, take a breath. Stop with the tantrums. Start making amends.

Making amends. What better place than the golf course to begin the process of making amends? The surroundings are beautiful. You come in contact with a finite number of people. The opportunities to say or do something uplifting roll on and on. The results of improved relationships can be seen immediately. The reinforcement is there. Think of it. The rituals of golf, the frequency of golf, the goals of golf. The generations of golfers all devoted to the same game, the same rules. It has all the makings of a tribe. And I don't mean tribe in the voyeuristic, made-for-TV, backbiting pseudo-survivor shows. I mean tribe in the most positive sense: caring people who associate by choice, contribute to the group as a whole, improve as individuals on their own and through association with others, and consciously acknowledge their responsibilities toward developing new members, whether they are children on their way to adulthood within the tribe or adults newly brought to the fold.

With all there is to like about golf, why not help to weed out what's not to like? At a minimum, make sure you're not enabling those ever-present Golfers from Hell who work hard to ruin their game and others' games or days. Further, make sure you're not cultivating new Golfers from Hell on your course or elsewhere. Instead, what about helping others discover this most positive of addictions?

Golf as an Antidrug?

I'm a big advocate of taking young people to the golf course and encouraging them to experience the game in all its glory and complexities. And I've certainly seen and experienced the joys of parents on the course with their children, celebrating the game and their time together. With instruction or guidance that is appropriate to the age (and absolute avoidance of imperious directives), everybody wins. There you are, with what seems like all the time in the world, open space, exercise—and a captive audience. What lessons you fit into that time are up to you. Out there, you've got nothing but teachable moments. A blank slate, good intentions, some cooperation from the Golf Gods, and who knows what can happen.

I know I've learned a ton from those night golf games with Scarlett and Paige. And they've learned as much about the community and support of golf from those laughter-filled evenings as they might have from weeks of serious lessons and enforced drills. More, no doubt. Without the pressure of an individual score and with the purpose very clearly designed as fun, they'll be coming back for more. Is it like the old dope peddler offering up the first highs for free? Well . . . you could say that. But then look at the benefits. And as you do, bear in mind that these benefits apply to children, siblings, spouses, other relatives, friends. All generations can share in the game, and all generations can learn more about the game and about each other. Later steps focus more on the possible links between finding good parenting moments and golfing. Here, we start with a few pieces of the foundation.

Life Lessons on the Course (Part One)

To my mind, golf gets a bad rap about taking time away from the family. It's not golf's fault when that happens. The game itself is very family friendly and can be an enormous boost. Just think of three possible gifts that can come through golf: time, lessons, and love.

Time. In today's busy life, many of us don't make enough time for what may well be our most important role: parenting. Or grandparenting. Or uncling or aunting. Funny, isn't it, that those last two aren't even words. Kids need all these people in their lives, and more. They need plenty of people who take active interest in their lives.

Is your role with the children in your life even on your calendar? Of course not, you may say; as a parent, it's a constant. Less so as a grandparent; maybe even as a favorite aunt or uncle. But what if you don't guard your time so you're sure to save good chunks of it for spending with those kids? What use is your wealth or success if your child, or a child in your life, is en route to becoming an ill-adjusted adult in the world? No matter what your role, what if you thought of your contribution to the next generation as the most important project of your life? As a parent, that's quite literally true. For many, many years, you and only you (together with your loving spouse, if you're lucky) are completely responsible for a human being, in every way.

Make sure that this project is a success. Put in as much time as required to ensure that your child is loved, listened to, is more important than anyone else. Time is the best investment you can ever make and the most precious gift you can give your child. And think of all the time you have together, uninterrupted, on the golf course!

Lessons. As parents, don't we all hope our kids will learn from the mistakes some other parents' kids make? I know my parents wished (quite vocally) that I had learned from the whopping mistakes the neighborhood kids made when I was growing up. But no, I had to try some of those mistakes on for size. We all did. But really, why?

On the golf course, it's different. Isn't it easy to break apart someone else's swing (only in your mind, of course, without your mouth engaged) and see just what they're doing wrong? If only it were just as easy to take those lessons and glue them onto your own knuckleheaded swing. But nobody's perfect. The good news is that golf and life provide enough examples for us to look around and learn. Learn from mistakes others make. Share your experiences—good and bad. Ask for help when faced with a tough situation. Chances are, you'll get good advice, advice that will go a long way in presenting you with alternatives to handle the situation—whether it's on the golf course or in life. And you'll be demonstrating some very important skills, skills that the children around you will absorb like a sponge does water.

Love. It's not enough to just love, it's important to show it. Seeing their parents in love as well as showering love on them wraps children in security, for the moment and for the future. Every positive and cheerful conversation in the house makes children comfortable and secure knowing that their home has harmonious vibrations. It sends children out into the world knowing that there is a safe haven for them. That there is a safe place to come back to, tired from the day's struggles, where they will be loved and cherished, no matter how bad the day may have been. And positive and cheerful conversations out on the golf course, facing the hardest game there is? That's love in the face of adversity!

Time, lessons, and love. Makes for a strong foundation. Mix it together with a tribe of supportive people, and they should easily balance out a lot of the challenges life may throw on the path through life. And if you can contribute to getting children on a good path, one without dead ends or landmines—all while enjoying a good round of golf with them—why not? Certainly it's a much more productive experience for all if they stay away from detours and dead ends, many of which wind up as the land mines of addictions. And I'm not talking about an addiction to golf.

Musings Between Holes

Recovering from alcoholism is a daunting and life-changing journey. It's also never-ending: it does not stop with the mere act of "putting a plug in the jug." Even if the plug stays put and they never again drink alcohol, other risks await alcoholics. If they are not extremely careful and meticulous about their programs, alcoholics run the risk of shifting one addiction to another. Many fall by the wayside, stone cold sober, as they spiral downwards, God forbid, into any of myriad other addictions, including gambling, sexual addiction, drug use, or eating disorders.

One "happy" addiction, however, is golf. To my knowledge, nobody ever died or ended up in jail because of their consumption with golf. Take my friend Arthur.

Slender, tightly wound, intense, and intellectual, Arthur is a professional, in the early stages of recovery from alcoholism. He views his weekly golf matches with his friends as vital to his recovery. This, in spite of the fact that he openly admits to trouble avoiding the nineteenth hole at his club, where he used to be known as a loud, boisterous, heavy-drinking know-it-all.

Now three years into recovery, he shakes his head in shame and embarrassment as he walks past the bar. He still sees and recognizes a few of his past drinking companions, but, like many recovering alcoholics, he acknowledges and accepts those "friendships" as hollow and to be avoided at all costs.

His alcoholism has cost him his marriage of twenty years, and he and his ex-wife still have a bumpy road ahead as they navigate shared parenthood of their fourteen-year-old son. Sadly, the ripple effect has shown up in this boy, who is acting out with his own tormented deeds. While addiction did not cost Arthur his job in high tech, he struggles with loneliness as he works diligently through the steps of his AA program. He treasures his weekly golf foursome as a refreshing respite from the rigors of recovery, and he brings passion and joy to the sport. His attitude is particularly refreshing, given that he is the first to recognize that his golf game is greatly flawed. Instead of bemoaning his game or giving up, he's tackling his game's weaknesses with the same diligence and positive energy as he tackled his alcoholism.

Those of us who love him have watched him progress, through golf, from a self-loathing, self-pitying, self-absorbed, and bitter individual into a gracious, giving, humble man who is learning to share his journey with others in an attempt to make reparations for the sins of his disease. We encourage him through our friendship; we embrace his reentry into the true challenges of reality, not the false delusions of addiction. Golf is the vehicle whereby Arthur is reconstructing his once-shattered life. He plays the game with care and respect, hole by hole, much as his AA program calls for one-day-at-a-time dedication.

In our minds, there is no more noble way for our friend to reclaim his life and revitalize his spirits. And—by the way—even on bad days, we never, *never*, patronize him, give him strokes, breaks, or mulligans. We didn't in the beginning, back when he was still drinking, and we don't now. Good thing, too, for in his newfound health has shaved five strokes off his score. As one of my other friends laments, in jest: "This is enough to drive *me* to drink!"

The Secret

The easy camaraderie of golf can, at its best, get us out of our own heads to see who's hurting around us—and do something about it. We can focus on life's little things and make small gestures of care. Without looking for results, we can simply know that kindness, while good in and of itself, will definitely have a ripple effect. The greatest power we have as humans is when we reach out to touch others. Could the secret be any simpler? *Care about others.* And, really, it's a two-way secret. As the Dalai Lama has said, "If you want others to be happy, practice compassion. If you want to be happy, practice compassion."

We are so incredibly blessed by nature's bountiful forces. Use golf as a canvas upon which to paint the best parts of your life. Use the sunshine of your giving self to sprinkle a little joy and levity upon the struggles of others, whether on the golf course or not.

> *"Instead of battling, embrace and accept."*
>
> — Bruce Lietzke

9

Pay Attention and Make Amends

S O NOW YOU'RE WILLING TO MAKE AMENDS, AND THE SECRET OF CARING about others is in your ears. What next? Next, in AA is this: *Made direct amends to such people* [meaning those you had harmed] *wherever possible, except when to do so would injure them or others.*

How do you make amends to all those golf partners, past and present? How do you minimize the amends you'll have to make to golf partners of the future? What about your partner at home? Mini-golfers at home? Power golfers at college? Oh, and that crew in the office that you deserted? And the conference participants who missed you at their table at the tag end of that last meeting? You remember the conference: the one when the weather was absolutely perfect and your golf clubs beckoned? Let's give it a try:

> *Fully aware that the Golf Gods know just how many people to whom we need to make amends, that they will uncover more and more people (and even entire categories of people) to whom we should attend, we take a deep breath, open our arms to the sky, and begin. There's no dodging the Golf Gods. And dodging those we've harmed just isn't working. So a little triage here. Look out for the ones who are still so pissed off at us that any*

attempt at redemption might ignite a fire. Work back to them.
First, get some practice by making amends to those who aren't
still steamed.

Let go, let golf.

AA on the Course and Across the Board

AA on the course? Clearly, it's not unheard of. But in this case, the double
A stands for Attention and Amends. How you can pay attention and make
amends on the links and beyond? Sometimes it's a way of being; sometimes
it's a way of thinking. And some places seem to make it easy. To my mind,
a golf course is one of them. Ireland is absolutely one of them.

Kaitlin Moira Siobhan. My wife Kate is as Irish as you'll find. Second generation, classic Irish looks, and the oldest of twelve, Kate has been back to
climb, walk, and bike in Ireland fifty times in her life. Fluent in Irish and in
the culture, she likes to say that "The bog holds the collective unconscious
of the Irish people." True or not, it is a remarkable country. On the first
of our many trips to Ireland together, I found myself sitting in a pub with
Kate's great-uncle John. I was still getting the hang of his lilting Irish brogue
when he asked me what I thought of the Irish. My answer, that everyone was
friendly and smiling, brought a huge smile to his face in return. He took a
deep breath and treated me to this Irish expression: "A smile is a beacon
to strangers and a resource unbound, can neither be begged, borrowed,
nor stolen. It's only of value when given freely. And those that have none
to give need one most of all. So remember that you can brighten another's
path with your smile."

Granted, it's not all about smiling. Those you've wronged are going to need
more than that. But there are plenty of reasons that we all recognize a smile,
across cultures and across countries. And there are plenty of reasons that
this moment in Ireland with Kate's Uncle John often comes back to me on
the golf course. I remember well how it feels to be surrounded by smiles

and friendship. And I consider myself fortunate to be able to recall such moments, to really feel them again, pretty much at will. Fortunate because sometimes basking in a smile is the perfect balm. It can't fix that bad slice, it can't find a ball lost in the rough, but it can put those things in perspective. It can keep a bad shot from precipitating a downward spiral on the course. For me, at least, it can be the first step in just shaking it off. And even simply remembering to shake it off starts me on the path to making amends with myself. I stop bad-mouthing myself under my breath or in my head. That done, it's easier to start anew with the next shot and to practice—and model—making amends with others. One mistake is not the end of possibilities. Not on the course and not with friends. And even multiple mistakes can be corrected and the damage undone enough for a new start.

And if, in the course of correcting your own mistakes, you're modeling a way that might work for others, you're not just making amends, you're helping others avoid the mistakes that would later warrant amends. Talk about a time-benefit ratio!

Life Lessons on the Course (Part Two)

The best instructors model perfect swings, perfect golf etiquette, perfect course management (in the sense of choosing the best route to the hole), and perfect manners. As importantly, they do it in such a way that people want to emulate them. So when you're the pro in your venue (as in the parent in a foursome, the old-timer in a group of new golfers), why not do the same, or as much of it as you possibly can? Three areas to focus on (in addition to the three touched on back in the previous chapter): stick with it, stay calm, really *be* the pro.

No, I'm not suggesting that you suddenly switch careers and become a golf pro. Nice as the fantasy may be, it's not in the range of reality for most of us. But the fact is, even those on the professional golf circuit and those who teach golf don't do everything right, every single time. They know what works for them and can execute that most of the time. The good instructors play a good game, but they make their living by analyzing someone's swing and game in a hurry and pointing people in the right direction. Incremental steps, and we can all take on that role.

Stick with it. Many times we are too tired, tired of the day's struggles, tired of the negativity we face with others, too tired to hang in there and do our best. But every time we give up, we teach just the wrong lesson: "Take the easy way out." Set an example of persistence by focusing on completing the task well, despite distractions or failures. Children are like elastic bands. They stretch you to the max, trying in every which way to see how much can you take. It may be frustrating, exasperating. It may seem as though they're baiting you, daring you to fail. But don't give in. The subtle power struggle that you face every day with your children is a test in itself for you. Each day you pass the test, you win the admiration of your children. And by watching you persist, they learn to overcome their daily struggles and be victorious in life. To varying degrees, the same goes for any new golfers you may be trying to bring along. You may not be perfect (who is?) but you love the game and life. Clearly it's worth the effort.

Stay calm. Sure, sometimes it might be tempting to just let it all out, to succumb to a tantrum of sorts. Surely it'd be easier to just get loud and angry, to let the storm come and roll over us, washing it away. But on the golf course? Really. You just look out of control, and is that what you want washing over the course? Do you really think it improves your game? And at home? If you shout at your children, get irritated with them and punish them physically when they disobey, what happens to them? What is the message you are sending? If you yourself cannot control your own temper, how can you expect your child to do so? If you—the big, strong, powerful grownup—don't count to ten, don't find a way to calm down, how can you expect your child to do so? Sure, it's hard sometimes. But if you don't control your temper, how can your child see any benefit in making the effort? Instead, what about really *being* that pro?

Be the pro. Be the role model. If you intend to impart certain values, make sure you follow them. Make sure you embody them. All the time. There are no vacations from values. If you truly value honesty, make sure you are honest yourself, in every way. Every day. In every circumstance. No fudging on the golf course, in the clubhouse, in the boardroom, at home. If you stress the importance of hard work, make sure you work hard too, at home and at work. You have the potential to be the best of examples for people in your orbit. And the worst example for your child. And the most influential person, too. As a mentor or as a parent, be conscious of the influence you have and the power of every action. Imagine that you have fresh, wet clay in your hand. How you mold it determines how it will last a lifetime, despite pressures from the world outside. My grandfather always told me that the loudest statement you can make about the world you envision is what you do in your own life. Can't argue that one. Seems straightforward, but—like golf—the actual practice is tricky and a challenge for a lifetime.

Musings Between Holes

Remember San Geronimo Golf Club, the course that Bob Hope golfed via limo? It may look gentle and rolling, but it's a surprisingly difficult layout nestled in the bucolic hills of West Marin. Located roughly midway between the town of Fairfax and the Pacific Ocean, this eighteen-hole head-scratcher is etched into the contour of Marin's fabled hillsides. If any of the landscape looks familiar, it's probably because one of the club's relatively close neighbors is Skywalker Ranch, the workplace of George Lucas and his far-reaching band of employees. Some of the live oak and redwood groves in the vicinity have been used as backdrops and specific scenery in the internationally acclaimed Star Wars movies.

When I say the course is "surprisingly difficult," it is because, at first glance, it looks fairly manageable. Not much water on the course, not overwhelming in distance or complexity. But . . . when the fog rolls in, when the winds howl, when the midsummer sun creates a mind-numbing hypnosis of the spirit, this idyllic place transforms into something distinctly non-idyllic.

San Geronimo can take on a lot. It was even the venue for a wonderful Coca-Cola commercial that has aired sporadically over the years. The commercial features a young boy playing golf by himself in the wee hours of the morning. Elegantly filmed, the ad captures dawn's eerie solitude, showing the young golfer trudging along the dew-soaked fairways. Water sprinklers arc lazily in the distance.

The kid approaches a par-three, swings earnestly, and watches in utter amazement (and apparently completely alone) as the ball lands softly on the green and plops into the hole for an ace. The kid's look is one of unabashed astonishment; then he looks around wildly in hopes that someone else may have witnessed this hallmark event. As he approaches the cup to fetch his ball, a course marshal riding a golf cart appears in the background. The marshal calls out: "Nice shot, kid! Of course, you know what this means?" The kid smiles broadly, and beams: "Yep, I am buying!" The shot fades to the two of them hoisting a bottle of Coke together. A moment is captured.

The Secret

Despite the image of a boy playing golf by himself (as many of the best golfers have, by the way) the story actually hinges on the connections and the traditions that are nurtured through golf. Even the young boy knew the two tribal rules about getting a hole in one: you need a witness, and you need to treat others to a drink. In this case, of course, a soda fit the advertiser's requirement, just as it also fit the boy's. And the promoters of Coca-Cola were, obviously, looking for both the cute factor and to link their drink to a celebration of achievement and good times, across generations. The golf tradition itself underscores this step's secret: *Be connected to family and community.*

Tiger Woods's late father, Earl, frequently stated that Tiger's true greatness far exceeds the golf course. His son's global awareness, manifested in his work with children, positions him as a mentor with platinum credentials. Let us benefit from his example by staying in touch with friends and family, checking in frequently, and making our presence a good thing. Practice listening actively. It's the reaching out that marks the depth of your character. What's a sure-fire way to connect and converse with a person or with a group? Inquire about the person's welfare. Really mean it, and listen to the answer. Don't worry about it being reciprocated; just know that you will get the attention you need and deserve in due time. In the meantime, through your efforts, you strengthen the entire tribe—on the course and off.

"A kid grows up a lot faster on the golf course. Golf teaches you how to behave."

— Jack Nicklaus

Play It Right and Play It Forward

S O, MAKING AMENDS ISN'T THE END OF IT. WE ALL KNOW IT'S A TWELVE Step program. In AA, the process continues, cycling back on itself. Step Ten? *Continued to take personal inventory and when we were wrong promptly admitted it.*

I guess you could think of the steps in total as round upon round of golf. You know the rules, you know the game, and still there are always new factors. And new twists to consider. And so,

> *We vowed to continue to take personal inventory and, where we were wrong, promptly shout it out to the heavens. Did we cheat on the scorecard? Did we kick a ball from the rough into the fairway? Did we mentally wish an opponent bad luck? Did we deliberately create a spike mark in front of his ball on the green? All these infractions and any of their ilk invite the wrath of the Golf Gods, purveyors of karma. We promised to play the game the way it was invented, fair and clean, giving the control and power back to those who invented it. Better yet, what more noble way is there to make amends than to pass on all of golf's greatness to our friends and children?*

Let go, let golf.

A Brief History

Play the game the way it was invented? Beyond fair and clean, this discussion won't go quite that far back. Just partway. While the '50s may seem like ancient history now, for those of us coming of age in the '50s and '60s, golf was a faraway, male-dominated venture shrouded in mystery and exclusivity. From a kid's perspective, the sport served as an escape hatch for dads. And as an elite networking venue. Both mostly for men. Yes, there were women who golfed, but—at least at many clubs—the days they were "allowed" on the course were restricted, and the most favored tee times went to men. No questions; no exceptions. Some children took lessons, but, again, their times on the course were severely restricted. Except for those children who came from families of golfers and belonged to a club, the closest most kids usually came to a golf course was if they worked as a caddy. And there were strict rules and attire even for that.

Country clubs in the '50s were the domain of the wealthy. And that's not the full story. Many clubs admitted only the very wealthy and the old money. The atmosphere was a bit rarefied. Not everywhere, but in enough places that the sport carried an air of exclusivity if not downright entitlement.

To my mind, a really wonderful thing about golf in the twenty-first century is that it has evolved into a more democratic engagement than ever before. Golf's explosion has turned it into a very cool enterprise on many levels, and one that reaches a much broader spectrum of people. But in those days, generally the only kids playing the sport in high school were the offspring of the rich. Naturally so, for most of the teams that existed were in wealthy communities. And even there, the kids who didn't golf viewed members of a high school's golf team as strange outsiders, maybe even geeks and dorks by more current terminology. Fact is, golfing was considered about as cool as stamp collecting.

The tide started changing with the surging popularity of Jack Nicklaus and Arnold Palmer in the early '60s. Nicklaus and Palmer possessed movie star charisma, and, with the burgeoning popularity of sports coverage on TV, they became the signature symbols for a sport that was suddenly becoming glamorous. Then, when a young teenage amateur named Johnny Miller thrilled the galleries at the U.S. Open at San Francisco's Olympic Club in 1964 by competing head-to-head with the likes of Nicklaus, Palmer, and Billy Casper, the youth stampede was on. Telegenic, irreverent, and looking very ungeeklike, Miller was one of the first of a new generation of golfers who signaled to the nation's young that the sport could, indeed, be very cool.

That trend has continued over the years and picked up speed. Think, for instance, of all that Tiger Woods has done for the popularity of the sport and for encouraging young people to take up the game. And they've done so in force. *Golfweek* magazine lists and ranks nearly three hundred college golf teams in the United States. Just Google "high school golf," and you'll find teams and clubs across the country—and around the world.

As a late-to-the-game golfer, I'm envious of the advantage these kids will have, thanks to growing up in the game. You can always spot those who started playing early: their swings are confident, relaxed, and natural—for it all *feels* natural to them. But obviously you can't just put a club in a two-year-old's hands and expect a Tiger Woods to emerge on the other side. From a young age, Tiger dreamed of being the world's best golfer. As he has written on his TigerWoodsFoundation.org site, he "worked hard and applied my family's values to everything I did. Integrity, honesty, discipline, responsibility, and fun: I learned these values at home and in school, each one pushing me further toward my dream."

And those values were clearly in play on the golf course, even as Earl Woods worked with his very young son. As David Owen wrote in Sidorksy's *Golf's Greatest Moments,* what Tiger's parents had in mind "was not to turn Tiger into a professional golfer, but to strengthen his character." As Earl Woods explained, the truly important lessons "on the golf course had to do not with swinging but with things like honesty, etiquette, patience, and discipline—virtues for which golf provided handy talking points." Talking points, teachable moments, golf instruction, life's lessons: it's clear Tiger absorbed them all.

There is only one Tiger. (Then again, he does have two children, and counting.) But even if neither parent nor child has his or her heart set on championship golf, think of the personal and emotional advantage available to new generations of parents and children—just by playing golf together.

Parenting on the Golf Course

While it's human nature that kids would probably prefer to play with their peers and adults would feel more comfortable in foursomes with people their own age, I happen to believe that golf is an absolutely wonderful bonding mechanism for mothers, fathers, sons, and daughters. In today's souped-up age of technological gimmickry that too often winds up—ironically—as a barrier to communication rather than a facilitator, what better way to get to know your kids than by an enjoyable day walking the fairways (and even the sand traps), enjoying each other, and talking about life, school, career?

Kids love this kind of inclusion. Even today, there's still a certain sense of awe they harbor about golf as a ritual for adults who have succeeded in life. Being invited into this world by their own parents gives them a feeling of belonging and esteem. They also get to view their parents in totally different surroundings. The leisurely setting is much more conducive to fluid conversation than the confining quarters of a kitchen table, a study, or an office. At the golf club, kids see their parents in a social atmosphere where other adults greet them with respect and conviviality. True, some of that happens on the sidelines at the kids' games, but there, the parents are fans and facilitators rather than participants and competitors—and kids know the difference. Nothing goes unnoticed in the eyes of curious young people, who suddenly have the experience of Mom and Dad being accepted and being considered—could it possibly be—*cool* by others. When their parents are happy and relaxed and feeling comfortable in their own activities, suddenly there is less pressure on kids. It makes interaction easier and enables them to share their thoughts and feelings more freely.

And what could be a better vehicle than golf for even the most hardened and cynical kids to view their parents struggling so mightily with the toughest sport on earth? The experience becomes humanizing, and the kids start to see the very fallible efforts made by their most immediate role models. Chances are good that the kids become less prone to mocking and scorning the folks, seeing them so directly engaged in this consummate battle with the self. Small steps to new respect, granted, but progress, nonetheless.

No matter how alienated young people may feel from their parents in other aspects of their relationship, the desire to perform well in front of them on a golf course can be a powerful motivator. For many, it's more immediate and more potent than the desire to get good grades in school. At the end of the day, parents and children have seen each other in a totally different and refreshing light. And, even if that's all the positive growth that's been made, the experience leaves a lasting and progressive impression for all.

Life Lessons on the Course (Part Three)

Big picture, of course, there are unending lessons in the whole concept of golf as a metaphor for life. From how you approach the day, the game, and the ball; to what and how you share with others; to the character, respect, discipline, energy, and attitude you exhibit: it's all there. Three lessons were included in each of the previous two chapters; here are four more. At first take, these may seem more focused on working with children and teens, but don't be fooled. Use these lessons, and *everyone* benefits, no matter what their age or their connection to you. Even you. If you're going to be the role model, be the pro, that's where you start. Start with how you play golf with your child, and take it from there. What do children require? Patience, clarity, realism, and genuine praise. Sounds like what we all need.

Practice patience. Remember when you first learned something? Not just how to do something better, but how to do it at all. From learning how to speak to learning how to swing a club, did you get it right the first time? Chances are, your first babbling sounds were met with smiles, praise, and a lot of attention from your parents. And if you started golf with a good pro, the pro found something to praise in what you did. Even if you completely whiffed the ball, that praise felt good. And then, slowly, you built on what you'd learned, forming words and—finally—a decent swing. It's the same with everyone. And, particularly with children, when asked to do something repetitive (and what could be more repetitive than practicing a golf swing to get it right), children and teens naturally tend to lose interest. So the challenge is for us (as parents, as on-the-spot pros) to make the task interesting, to encourage and teach them to patiently work on it until they get it right.

Be absolutely clear. Clarity is tough. It requires forethought. It also demands that you not send mixed signals. Many parents learn this on the home front, sometimes the hard way, when their kids push the limits they've imposed. But out on the golf course, clarity can be a new challenge. How do you teach the rules that apply there and keep it fun? As with anything, modeling and consistency go a long way. And especially as you're starting out, it's a clean slate. If your children have watched televised golf matches with you, they may know a little something. But that would be a little something about championship play. The rest of us don't have an entourage, and we can't make those shots. Instead, we pull our own clubs from the bag and replace our own divots. That means you can't walk away from a divot. Not ever. And when your children make them, show how to replace them properly and help them do so. Don't step over one, not even "just this one time." If, between advice, divot repair, and questions, a foursome stacks up behind you, let them play through. Golf is not a game to be rushed. And neither is raising children. Don't plan on playing eighteen holes when you're first starting. Don't even plan on nine holes. In the beginning, why not plan on ending the round after just a few holes so the emotional and muscle memories are good ones. Build up to a full round. Throughout, be very clear. Clear about what behaviors and attitudes are commendable and which are not okay. Clear about the responsibility your child can shoulder. Your being clear will help your child be very clear in decisions in the future.

Be realistic. When you set a task for yourself, accomplish it, no matter how long it takes or how hard it is. Some of this speaks to the point in Step Nine about sticking with it. Closely connected is the need to set realistic goals. If you demonstrate setting realistic goals for yourself and challenging yourself with some reach goals, your children will pick up on it. You're realistic enough to know you're not going to have a second career on the pro golf circuit. But you can set golfing goals for yourself: you can strive to lower your handicap, bit by bit; you can study up on the course you'll play on vacation so you'll golf better and enjoy it more. Your children will see you set goals and break them into manageable chunks, maybe even ask for help doing the same. This is not to say that you push your children toward goals that are way beyond their capacity, but goals that are within their capacity and goals that require a little (or increasing) stretch of abilities will strengthen their resolve to succeed. Every goal achieved will help with the next one.

Praise. Praise your children early and often. On the golf course and off. There's a great bumper sticker that proclaims, "Children need encouragement, every day." It's true. And don't we all? Instead, many parents punish easily but don't praise that often. And why is that? Bad habits? Bad tape loops? Or do we really think that praise can go to the head? Think again. It is proven that genuine and sincere compliments, especially those received from parents, are the ones most cherished by children. Those compliments are a source of energy that enables them to aim higher and achieve more. Praise your children for effort taken, for hard work put in, for achievements, for good character, for good manners, and for empathy. Each bit of praise helps children learn to be gracious in success and to weather failures well—and we all have failures. Praise helps keep children balanced.

Musings Between Holes

Just for fun, imagine putting these lessons into practice as you're walking to the next hole with your foursome. As always, there will be plenty of banter. Certainly that last hole provided the fodder for a whole range of ribbings and jokes. But what about incorporating some patience, clarity, realism, and genuine praise in there too? What was it that looked right on that last green? Was one of your partner's putts an absolute beauty? Can you picture that and praise that? Done often enough and over time, your golfing buddies will understand that your praise is genuine and not some new bit of gamesmanship thrown out there to undermine their confidence. Who knows? Maybe it'll help break some adult habits and begin to improve everyone's game. Done right from the beginning with your children, praise will help them feel good about the game, their game, and themselves. And as for realism and clarity: yes, you know you still haven't got that chip shot down. That was crystal clear to everyone. Practice patience with yourself along the way. Don't let that one bad shot interfere with your next shots. You can always work on your chips on your own, or even get some expert help before your next round. Bit by bit, you'll get there.

The Secret

That expert help costs money. For that matter, golfing costs money, even without lessons. Equipment, greens fees; more equipment, more greens fees. It would be a shame to miss out on golf's many joys merely because we have not earned the money and learned how to manage it. And so, the secret: *save a little each month.*

Putting a portion of your earned money aside each time you are paid is a healthy discipline that teaches you how to value money while increasing your own sense of self-worth and discipline. Given the recent financial crisis, saving and living more frugally may be coming back into style. (Not that they ever went out of style with some people.) As Ben Franklin said, back in the 1700s: "If you know how to spend less than you get, you have the philosopher's stone." The philosopher's stone? Through the ages the philosopher's stone was considered to have the power to transmute base metals into gold; in more modern parlance, it's the shortcut to riches or even the elixir of life. On the most practical of levels, saving money requires self-reliance, teaches self-reliance, and supports self-reliance. And isn't self-reliance one of the most sublime and multifaceted lessons we attain from golf? Think about it: no one else can swing the club for you, or practice for you, or keep your thoughts calm through a competition. Off the course, you have to take your own tests, take responsibility for your thoughts, choices, and decisions—and accept the consequences. Self-reliance is critical to a life well lived. And wouldn't it be an asset in the world we live in today?

> *"Golf is the closest game to the game we call life. You get bad breaks from good shots; you get good breaks from bad shots; but you have to play the ball where it lies."*
>
> — Bobby Jones

STEP ELEVEN

Cultivate a Generous Mindset

MUCH OF STEP TEN, WHETHER FOR AA OR FOR GOLF, CYCLED BACK around the need to take constant inventory, admit to wrongs, and strive for better. Being the pro, being the constant and steadfast role model—whether on the course or at home—takes nonstop attention and effort. No wonder AA asks for some serious help in Step Eleven: *Sought through prayer and meditation to improve our conscious contact with God, as we understood Him, praying only for knowledge of His will for us and the power to carry that out.*

That role modeling, and constantly walking the talk—on the golf course and off—is hard. As if we didn't have enough details and corrections to think about while we were golfing? Never mind the social niceties; just what *did* the golf pro say to do with that right elbow? It's clear we're going to need help here, and not just from the golf pro, but from the big pros.

> *Through rigorous contemplation and soul-searching, we genuinely emptied ourselves of everything we ever thought we knew about golf and decided, albeit begrudgingly, to truly surrender our wills to the Golf Gods. That done, we hope they'll listen as we beseech them to finally reveal to us what in God's name we were supposed to be doing out there on the links all along. Goodbye, pride and braggadocio; hello, humility, goodness, generosity, grace, gratitude, and serenity.*

Let go, let golf.

In Golf and in Life, We Are Entitled To Exactly . . . Nothing

The golf of the old days, as mentioned in the previous chapter, is now ancient history. And good thing. The exclusivity of golf was just one example of the many polarizing experiences that were abundant in the extremely linear, one-dimensional, drably uninspired world we inhabited back then. And, yes, it's got a ways to go; and, yes, it's changing still.

One of the greatest lessons in life and in the ideals of democracy that have shaped America is the idea that we really are all created equal. Nobody is innately better than anyone else. (In the larger sense, not the golfing sense. On the golf course, I'm all too aware that when inborn abilities for golf were handed out, I didn't even know the line was forming.) What we do have are blessings of talent that can be extinguished as easily as they were inherited. And glimmers of talent that can yet be coaxed into something. In both cases, the good Lord gives, and the good Lord takes away, sometimes with breathtaking alacrity.

Our job with the talent we do possess is to work as hard as we can, do our very best, and neither be overly impressed with our achievements nor overly depressed about our shortcomings. The sooner we take up this job, wholeheartedly, the better off we will be. The sooner we fully understand that we have to earn, really earn, everything we need and want for ourselves and for others, the better off we will be. It's a cliché for a reason: there is no such thing as a free lunch. In this life and in the sport of golf, we reap what we sow. It's as simple as that.

And simple gets you there.

Keep It Simple, Stupid

Keep it simple, stupid. That's life boiled down to its barest essentials. That's golf reduced to its most sublime core. After all, aren't we all trying to live well, enjoy ourselves, and brighten the world a bit in the process? And isn't it the same in golf, but with the addition of chasing a tiny ball around a magnificent and huge course at the same time?

Consider the lovably simple soul that Tom Hanks played in the award-winning 1994 film *Forrest Gump*. In the movie, Gump sits on the bench at a bus stop, telling the story of his rather fascinating life to anyone sitting next to him. He is not a bright man, but he understands that, he has no pretenses, and everyone seems to like him. He takes life as it comes, remembering that as his mother told him, "Life is like a box of chocolates. You never know what you're gonna get." It sounds so utterly simple coming out of Gump's mouth. And the story, while layered, sticks with Gump's simplicity.

As a child wearing leg braces to correct his spinal curvature, Gump is constantly picked on at school. His only friend, Jenny, is a poor white-trash girl who we slowly realize is abused at home. Eventually, the two graduate from high school. Somehow Forrest manages to accidentally impress a college coach with his running ability (honed over many years of fleeing bullies while wearing the leg braces) and become a star running back on the college football team.

Upon graduation, the young Gump joins the Army, which is already embroiled in Vietnam. At basic training, Gump meets "Bubba" Blue, a poor black man whose brainpower seems roughly the same as Gump's. The two arrive in 'Nam and are met by their platoon commander, Lieutenant Dan Taylor, whose ancestors commanded and died in virtually every war America ever fought. During a particularly rough firefight, most of Gump's squad mates are wounded, and Bubba is killed. Using his amazing running talent, Gump carries the survivors (including Lieutenant Dan) to safety just before an air strike. In the process, Gump is wounded in the posterior. For his actions, he is given the Congressional Medal of Honor.

While recovering in the hospital, he begins an obsessive love of Ping-Pong. He eventually becomes so good at the game that he is sent to China to play against their finest players and becomes somewhat of a celebrity. Once he leaves the service, Gump fulfills his promise to visit Bubba's grave in Bayou Labatrie, Alabama, and buys a shrimp boat. Lieutenant Dan (whose legs were amputated as a result of his Vietnam injuries) joins Gump on the boat, and, after a rough start, their business becomes a huge success.

After the death of his doting mother, and another parting from Jenny (who rejected his proposal of marriage and then slept with him), Gump becomes dejected and starts running across America. Eventually, Gump crosses the country a couple of times. As an aside: I actually ran across the country, too, *twice*—honest!—and years before the movie. Not long after my runs, I hung up my running shoes and discovered golf. I had a team running with me and supporters behind the scenes, all with the goal of raising money and awareness for drug prevention. In contrast, Gump had no official cause, no support team, and he was trailed by masses of adoring fans who believed he was some kind of prophet. (I was never in that league. Not by a long shot.) Just as quickly as he made the decision to start running, Gump decided to stop and go home.

As these events (plus many additional accidental "historical encounters," like meeting JFK and Nixon in the White House) are happening, Jenny is seen in various scenes being expelled from college, taking up with counterculture types, and nearly committing suicide in the 1970s. Eventually Gump and Jenny are reunited. Their happiness is short-lived, though, as Jenny dies from an unnamed virus. In the end, Forrest is alone with his son, left to pass on his life's lessons.

No need to pontificate about the point. There are as many different views of this movie as there are viewers of it. And yet, it still holds up as a compelling, credible drama in an age of hideously vivid film violence and wanton crimi-nality. In my humble opinion, the movie gains traction by demonstrating and redemonstrating its central theme in various ways. As Gump's mother puts it, and as Gump clearly took to heart: "You have to do the best with what God gave you." That advice sure packs a lot into a few words.

Gump's generosity of spirit and simple generosity in all he did got him though some tough times and enabled him to help others along the way. And, yes, he's a fictional character. But as great writers through the years have proven time and time again, there's a lot to be learned in fiction.

Musings Between Holes

But wait, you say, didn't you pick up this book to learn about golf? Why all this discussion of a movie, and a simple one at that? The lessons are the same, in golf, in the movie, in life. In short, if we just focus on what we are doing in life, good things will come our way. It's as simple—and as difficult—as focusing on the shot you're facing. Not the one you just attempted. Not the one you know is coming up around that dogleg. The one in front of you now.

It's hard. Anyone who golfs knows. Anyone who practices meditation knows. Try to focus on one shot, on one thought, and suddenly a raft of other shots and thoughts come flying into view. It takes practice. Like any meditative experience, golf takes practice to build that muscle. The more you practice, the stronger it gets. Practice enough, and you can call up that calm strength whenever you need it.

I think often of my friend Master Vin, back from my days in Vietnam. In all the time we spent together, I never saw him when he wasn't fully present and aware. The surrounding circumstances were anything but calm—and he was fully engaged with his world, without a bit of denial. But no matter what was going on around him, he exuded calm strength. Calm strength and great joy. He had long since mastered the art of living in the moment and filtering out any thoughts that did not serve that moment well. What a golfer he might have been! And oh how he'd have laughed at the idea.

The Secret

Keeping an upbeat attitude and a calm presence are not just tools to make you feel good. They are tools that can improve the world. The secret? *Be generous with your positive spirit.* Let it draw people to you and let it shine on those around you.

Remember that Irish saying about the smile? This is really about sharing a much larger smile, the inner goodness of your being. Share in every way you can. Show compassion to strangers; express empathy toward a stressed-out store clerk. As American author and lecturer Leo Buscaglia put it, "Too often we underestimate the power of a touch, a smile, a kind word, a listening ear, an honest compliment, or the smallest act of caring, all of which have the potential to turn a life around." There are a lot of struggling souls in the world. There is no telling what a kind word can mean in the life of someone crying inside. Most importantly, it's the right thing to do. And, by the way, you will feel good doing it and feel better about yourself. It all makes for a good mindset, for golf and for life.

> *"For this game you need, above all things, to be in a tranquil frame of mind."*
>
> — Harry Vardon

STEP TWELVE

Celebrate Life!

WITH MASTER VIN AND KATE'S UNCLE JOHN IN MY HEAD, I NOW come to Step Twelve. Notice that although we're at the twelfth of twelve steps, in neither AA nor golf is there a final step: complete this and leave all the steps behind. The steps, as anyone in the AA program knows, are intimately connected to each other. And Step Twelve? *Having had a spiritual awakening as the result of these steps, we tried to carry this message to alcoholics, and to practice these principles in all our affairs.*

To practice these principles in all our affairs? In business, in life, even in golf? As I keep telling the ever-patient pro at the golf course: I'm trying, I'm trying. But just when, exactly, is that going to show up in my game, in the scorecard? It's ongoing, right? Never-ending. And then . . .

> *Like a lightning bolt (or a Titleist to the forehead), we suddenly reap the rewards of adhering to all the previous steps, and, in one crystal-clear moment, we come to the realization that every-thing we have newly learned about golf is precisely the same set of guidelines and discipline that we are now better prepared to bring to real life itself. I golf, I screw up, I make amends, I try again, I laugh, I cry, I pray, I curse, I love, I fall, I soar—therefore I am. Golf and life, interchangeable, all the same.*

Let go, let golf.

Live and Laugh (Versus Swing and Swear)

All too often, we really are our own worst enemies, both in life and in sport. We put too much pressure on ourselves. Instead of celebrating our God-given talents, we put them to shame when we stumble, and we brag overly much when we succeed. But why?

If you are prone to seeking complexity and making your life tough, take a breath. And then ponder this question: what were you thinking, choosing golf as a sport? Even if complexity is not your mindset, golf will make you crazy. Golf is a sport that screams for simplicity. Forget trying to be Arnold, Jack, Gary, Lee, Tiger, Phil. Instead, think Forrest Gump. Remember his mother's advice: "Life is like a box of chocolates. You never know what you're gonna get." If *life* is like a box of chocolates, *golf* is too—in certain ways. Much as you might like one, there certainly isn't a handy guide that tells you which chocolate—or stroke, or bit of luck—you'll get as you tee up. You just have to learn the basics, start playing, improve the basics, develop the skills, play some more—and then go with the flow as best you can. So instead of beating yourself up for not hitting like one of the pros, try to focus with the serene wholeness of a Forrest Gump or a Chauncey Gardner.

Forrest Gump and Chauncey Gardner? Who are they to be role models? What *am* I thinking?

In the 1979 film *Being There*, a simple-minded gardener named Chance has spent all his life in the Washington, D.C., house of an old man. When the man dies, Chance is put out on the street with no knowledge of the world except what he has learned from television—and from gardening. After a run-in with a limousine, he ends up a guest of a woman (Eve) and her husband, Ben, an influential but sickly businessman. Now called Chauncey Gardner, Chance becomes friend and confidante to Ben and an unlikely political insider who, with his ability to cut to the chase of all things, becomes a most sought-after consultant—all while staying utterly oblivious to self-importance.

Ah, the beauty of his simplicity. Played brilliantly by film legend Peter Sellers, Chauncey's seemingly simple mind appears to grow in depth with each encounter, and he gradually takes on the aura and mystique of a wise man on a mountaintop. Why? Simply because he has mastered the art of saying things with immense clarity, utterly devoid of double meaning, manipulation, or malice. The more crystalline and pure his thoughts and words, the more power and influence Chauncey commands, even though that is not his intent. It's something to think about the next time you are crowding your head with too many thoughts as you stand crouched over an insidious four-foot putt. Let go. Let golf.

From Being There to Being Here

The motto of the Jesuit priests, regarded by many as the wisest and worldliest of all clergy, is *Age quod agis*. Translated, the aphorism means "Do what you are doing." How's that for utterly boiled-down simplicity? Life's biggest lesson could not be distilled into any finer form. Do what you are doing, and the rest will be revealed. So many of us miss the whole concept, on the golf course and along life's choppy fairways. We thrash, we crash, we wallow, and we despair; we behave like powerless little creatures and all too often forget to reach deep inside ourselves for strength, peace, serenity, and love. But why? Why not instead simply ask for these things in our daily prayers, then let go of the search. Let go. Let golf.

Think about it. What we have day in and day out is the "moment" we live in; just that. So why not be *present* for it, embrace it, and enjoy it?

On the golf course, as in life, just do what you are doing, and do so for the sheer joy of living. The power that comes from adherence to this practice—be it in the joyous simplicity of your newfound golf swing or the passionate commitment to living well—forges a symmetry in your life and in your sport that can only be described as sheer happiness.

Grasping these tools in both life and golf is an act of enhanced consciousness that will radically improve your status as a person, an athlete, a friend, and a confidante. I emphasize, by the way, that we are all very mortal individuals, eternally in a state of flux, forever characterized as works in progress. The dynamic endorsed here is much like the oft-expressed therapeutic dictate that we should confront our fears head-on in order to move ahead. Facing our fears does not necessarily mean that we will conquer our fears, but it is in the process of facing them that we become better, stronger people. It's like the well-worn quote about life being not a destination but rather a journey. Look at Tiger Woods. Even the best there ever was is never fully satisfied and never will be. We learn so much more from our mistakes than we do from our successes. Once we learn to accept that and come to peace with reality, then we can start to make specific, targeted steps in the maturation of ourselves as people and, yes, as golfers. Let go. Let golf.

Musings Between Holes

Maturation. As people. As golfers. These are good things. And with that maturation, as you look around, you may begin to see that you *have* learned a few things, after all. Not everything there is to learn about golf. Certainly not everything there is to learn about life. But you have tucked away a few things that make a difference, both in life and in golf.

I'm far from a golf pro, by anyone's standards. I'm still working on improving my handicap. But the lessons about life that can sneak in on the golf course? The importance of optimism, integrity, hard work, respect, dedication, friendship, gratitude? I'm all over that.

And anytime I have the opportunity (whether it's as my golf ball is sinking to the bottom of a water hazard or as Kate and I make a periodic pilgrimage to Walden Pond with a few of our nieces and nephews), you can bet I'll take note of the ripples. How I react as my golf ball splashes down in the water—my body language, my words, and what I carry forward—says a lot. Can I be gracious, mentally file away what I miscalculated, what I did wrong on that stroke as a lesson for next time, and move on? Can I laugh at the ribbing I'll get from the rest of my foursome without secretly hoping for payback later? Can I still enjoy the beauty of that gorgeous windswept pond and not curse it as an infernal water hazard? Really? Can I take my own advice and shake it off, being genuinely happy that my biggest problems at the moment are a lost Titleist and an extra stroke? And as I toss a pebble in Walden Pond and watch the ripples, can I speak with honesty to the next generation about being conscious and aware of every action, knowing that what we do has direct and indirect effects on others? Even others we may never know? I can do my best, and I can remind my fellow travelers of Henry David Thoreau's words from "The Pond in Winter," a chapter from *Walden*: "If one advances confidently in the direction of his dreams, and endeavors to live the life which he has imagined, he will meet with a success unexpected in common hours." Advancing confidently in the direction of one's dreams. Now *there's* a goal for the ages. Can I play it forward and do my part to encourage those around me to do the same?

There's still plenty to learn, of course. And whatever course you're on, everything counts. Everything. Everything you do in your life, and everything you do that touches another. Again, that's everything. So whether you're aware of it then, now, or in the future, make sure all your ripples are good ones.

The Secret

To navigate any course—straightforward or devilishly hard—we need the awareness and discipline to be constantly vigilant, nurturing our personal lives and our golf routines. By minimizing our flaws and downplaying any personal annoyances, even tiny minor ones, we all are contributing to the greater good. And isn't that key, for all of us?

As we celebrate the conclusion of *Twelve Steps to Eighteen Holes*, my fondest wish is that you have come to understand the lessons of the Twelve Steps, and will hold them in mind as you wend your way through the fairways, the sand traps, the water hazards, and the greens ahead. And that you carry those steps with you even to the clubhouse, the nineteenth hole, and beyond. Golf is, after all, just one of the challenges you choose to take on, and the lessons are useful in all of life's challenges.

As others learn by example, they will notice your example and take steps to change themselves. As you stay informed on issues relating to your community, small and large, and make the extra effort to do something about those issues, others will too. You are what you do; we are all what we do. So let's make the words "do something" be part of our daily mantras.

The secret? *You can make a difference. Believe it, and you can make it happen.* With that secret (not really a secret, is it?) you can practice playing it forward, every day, every chance you get. Practice, and you can improve your game, your life, and who knows how many other lives along the way?

And so, I close this chapter with a quote that I consider a gift to me, perhaps from the Golf Gods themselves. I awoke from a dream with this repeating in my head: GOLF: Go, live fully; Go, live freely; Go, love forever. The details of the dream itself escaped me as I opened my eyes, but the phrase kept ringing in my ears. I rather liked the lilt of it and the repetition. And then I saw it:

GOLF: **GO,** *Live Fully;* **GO,** *Live Freely;* **GO,** *Love Forever.*

GOLF: GOLF, GOLF, GOLF!

Enjoy it. All the challenge, opportunity, struggle, accomplishment, beauty, glory, friendship, celebration, and ultimately the freedom. Out there on the links, out there in your life, enjoy it all—and pass it on.

Epilogue

Throughout *Twelve Steps to Eighteen Holes: Let Go, Let Golf,* I've repeated a few messages more than a few times. Believe me: it's not that I've forgotten; it's that I can't help but emphasize how important these connections are—to each of us as individuals, to each of us as golfers, to everyone who is part of the golfing tribe, to the broader community, to every single human being.

Golf is most extraordinary in the opportunities for community, for sharing, for the constant presence of moments to pass on lessons and learnings. The practical details about the course are the smallest of them all. But lessons on course management can translate into lessons on life management, on overcoming adversity, on building strength and character. Every single round, no matter the course, no matter the conditions, holds lessons about golf, about life.

My hope is that in these pages I've successfully conveyed at least some of the majesty and wonder of golf and how, in the bigger picture, it's about living life with character and responsibility. It's about living in the moment and taking steps for the future. And whether you have children of your own, nieces and nephews, goddaughters and godsons, grandchildren, students, employees, neighbors, friends, know that by sharing golf with them, you're sharing your life and helping them in theirs. You'll find that adding the spark of golf to someone's life leaves you with a great feeling.

And if you're looking for more ways to pass it on, whether on the golf course or out in life, I have another thought for you. Become part of an organized group working with the next generation. There are plenty of them out there, many in need of capable adults. Do I have a particular group in mind? You bet!

You already know that I've been in the mentoring field for many decades. Between working with substance abuse prevention, treatment, and recovery groups; serving on boards; and writing books, I've seen all sides of mentoring. I've seen programs around the globe and close to home. There are multiple governmental programs designed to address the four social epidemics facing young people: drug and alcohol abuse, teen pregnancy, gang participation, and dropping out of school. Yet the problems persist. They persist despite staggering quantities of slogans, pamphlets, videos, and public service announcements, all designed to steer kids in positive directions. They persist despite the best intentions of presenters who talk to kids. Why? There are lots of reasons but, as any parent knows, talking *to* kids has limited benefit. It's the talking *with*, the actively participating *with* kids that makes a difference. That's part of what talking on the golf course accomplishes. It's the being involved *with* kids, actively mentoring them, that shows results, on the course and in life.

As you'd expect, we're big on mentoring at the California Mentor Foundation. And we paid attention when mentoring leaders reported that recruitment and retention were their top challenges. The real news came when we learned of the numbers of people who said they would become mentors if the process could include a game plan for each young person's future.

What? A game plan for life? A way for mentors to help young people create meaningful life competencies? A process for improving vision, insights, and abilities in areas like financial literacy, decision making, study skills, health and nutrition, career planning, and values? Sounds like a Lifeplan.

Through the Lifeplan Institute, we've mobilized an entire tribe of Lifeplan experts, trainers, and facilitators—all of whom are passionate about helping children and young adults and committed to the idea of making the world a better place. Our goal is to reach ten million youths and young adults in ten years—and help them become successful, thriving adults. If you'd like to join us in this quest and become a mentor in an ever-growing network, in person and online, you'll be paying it forward well beyond the golf course, for years to come. Just think of the size of those ripples!

To contact Lifeplan, see our website (www.lifeplaninstitute.org), or send an e-mail to info@lifeplaninstitute.org, and we'll get you started.

Golf Glossary Giggles

Golf clichés, sayings, and affirmations are plentiful and colorful, but what has always struck me is how closely they reflect what is going on in our own lives. If playing golf is a never-ending enterprise that is constantly changing and revealing, exactly the same can be said of real life. Let's see how some terms from golfing are useful in both golf and life.

Bogey. Golfers in the United States know this term (all too well) as one over par for any one hole. But a quick trip to the dictionary tells a longer story. Webster's first definition? Specter, phantom. Second? A source of fear, perplexity, or harassment. Now *that* explains a lot. Don't all golfers live in fear of bogeys? But, according to Webster, it's not until the third definition that golf comes specifically into focus:

> 3. a. *chiefly Brit*: an average golfer's score used as a standard for a particular hole or course
>
> b. one stroke over par on a hole in golf (*Merriam Webster's Collegiate Dictionary*, 11th ed.)

And then comes the final definition: a numerical standard of performance set up as a mark to be aimed at in competition. I'm not aiming for a bogey in competition, but maybe they are on the other side of the pond.

Clenching. This may be the opposite of allowing your "swing to swing itself." Clenching can be focusing so hard on each of the individual components of a "natural" swing that the result becomes anything but natural. Picture it in another sport: If you're out on the ski slopes, and it's cold and you clench, what happens? You get colder. Relax. Breathe. Unclench. This is fun, remember?

Course Management. Also "game management," the use of strategy, or a thoughtful plan, emphasizing strengths and accommodating weaknesses to make one's way around a golf course, as opposed to haphazardly hitting the ball and chasing it. Living life haphazardly can be a dangerous, frustrating, exhausting, and damaging experience. Since most of us aren't given a life plan strategy, we have to dig deep with discipline and come up with our own set of goals to help us achieve independence and happiness in life. Playing and living with utter abandon can be fun, wild, and exhilarating for a while, but to consistently ignore the obstacles and willfully proceed without some kind of strategy is usually a recipe for failure.

Golfer. I'm told that in calculating the number of golfers (and potential audience for its magazine), *Golf Digest* defines *golfer* as anyone who has a set of clubs and plays golf at least four times a year. *Golf Digest* says nothing about how old those clubs are or what kind of shape they're in. Neither does it address how often a golfer thinks about playing, hopes to play, watches tournament play, or dreams about playing even half as well as the pros. But take heart: only 10 percent of those who play golf have broken 90. Ever. *See* **Optimist**.

Go to School. To learn from another player's shot, most commonly associated with putting, seeing how a putt on a similar line to your own will break. Never underestimate the influence of others' behavior on our own. Choose your role models and mentors wisely, emulate their best qualities, and you will be certain to gain positively from the experience.

Grind. Maintaining or intensifying one's mental focus, similar to the expressions "bear down" or "stay focused"—generally meaning to concentrate on every shot and not get distracted. In life, the secret to success depends on grinding. There may be occasional spurts of glory and days that are spiked with monumental personal triumphs and celebrations, but, for the most part, we gain persistence, patience, prosperity, and pride by the often humdrum commitment to the everyday tasks and challenges that will ultimately lead to a life well lived.

Mulligan. Also known as "breakfast ball," "lunch ball," and "Sunday ball." These are all terms for taking a second attempt, replay, "do-over" at a shot when one doesn't like the result of the first attempt. Mulligans simply don't exist in professional golf and in regular matches by serious-minded players who adhere religiously to the strict and sacred rules of the game. But in casual, friendly play, a mulligan is probably the only nod ever given to the more human side of golf. Most players who grant mulligans never allow more than one or two over the stretch of eighteen holes. In real life, we really don't get mulligans with most of our major decisions, but who among us doesn't cry on occasion for a second chance with a boss, a mate, a parent, or an officer of the law?

Nassau. Not the place, the bet. If you have to ask, you may not want to play. But, really, it's simple. Except it consists of three separate bets: one for the front nine, one for the back nine, and one for the overall eighteen holes. The player with the lowest score on a hole wins a point; if there's a tie, it's considered a "push"—no points gained or lost for anyone. If you're losing the Nassau at the end of the front nine, you might "press" the bet, giving yourself a double-or-nothing chance at coming out ahead. A friendly Nassau might be a $2 bet; more than that, and who can concentrate on the game? And would you have enough money left over to pay for a round if you get that elusive hole in one?

Never Up, Never In. Refers to the obvious fact that if a putt does not have enough speed to reach the hole, it can't go in. Probably the best practitioner ever of this simple golf philosophy is Arnold Palmer, who is the very personification of boldness, smart risk taking, and the pulsating spirit of devil-may-care bravado, all of which earned him the nickname "Charging Arnie." His theory on putting has always been that if the ball doesn't roll past the hole, it never has a chance of going in. Living bold, letting people know who you are in vivid, clear strokes of self-expression is an admirable, courageous way to live. Good fortune always seems to come to those who play and live with a brave sense of throwing caution to the wind. But to have that appearance, to get the luck, they've done the hard work first.

Optimist. That would be you. Think about it: you have to be an optimist to play golf. In what other sports are the odds so stacked against the participant? In what other sport is the venue designed to be so challenging, so changing, so dependent on the weather and the Golf Gods? Sure, once in a while you hit a shot that feels perfect—and even lands where you'd wanted it. And, as Robert Sidorsky wrote in *Golf's Greatest Moments*, "There is some truth to the old adage that it takes only one good shot to bring us back to the course, but the lure of golf goes much deeper. Golf is a game for optimists, or perhaps it would be more accurate to say that it appeals to the optimistic side of our nature while never quite fulfilling it."

Speed Golf. Really. I'm not making this up. Speed golf is rumored to have started in California in the late '70s and has spread since then, with waves of ever-younger runners. The goal is to complete a round of golf in the lowest combination of strokes and time. Players run between shots, carrying their own clubs (from as few as one to as many as six). And, no, there's not extra credit for carrying extra weight. It's just shots and time to completion. Oh, and there's no slacking: speed golfers have to fix their ball marks, rake sand traps, and conform to the other niceties of golf. Except they can putt without removing the flagstick. That can save on time—if there's not a rebound.

Waggle. Some kind of motion or movement. Can be very individualized, but many times a back-and-forth movement at the hands or wrists while holding the club. The purpose? Staying loose, feeling the club, keeping the body in motion instead of holding still. Waggles start out intentional and can quickly become habits. Good ones? You be the judge.

Yips. The involuntary, apparently uncontrollable twitches of the hands or lower arms that cause golfers to blow simple putts. The jury is out on the cause: could be psychological (they often occur when the pressure is on), could be purely neuromuscular (they involve intricate, delicate movements), could be both. Could be simply revenge of the Golf Gods, for all we know.

Index

About the Author

As a relatively new convert to golfing, Andy Mecca is more than avid about it. But then, he brings that kind of energy to everything, whether it's participating in sports, working to prevent drug abuse, mentoring youths and adults, even running across the country.

Mecca, who received his master's and doctorate in public health from the University of California, Berkeley, currently serves as President of the California Mentor Foundation and as the Co-founder and Chief Inspiration Officer of Lifeplan Institute, whose purpose is to help adolescents and young adults actively plan their ways to thrive now and in the future.

A respected drug treatment professional for forty years, Mecca served as California's Drug Czar from 1991 to 1998. Mecca was Executive Director of the California Health Research Foundation from 1978 to 1991 and served as the Chair of the California Commission on Improving Life Through Service in 1994. He was also the Chairman of the California Task Force on Self-Esteem, which released its final report in 1990. The Task Force achieved a fleeting kind of fame by being featured in *Doonesbury*, Garry Trudeau's cartoon strip.

From 1975 to 1986, Mecca was Chief of Alcohol and Drug Services in Marin County, in the San Francisco Bay Area. He directed the Army's Drug Treatment Program in Vietnam from 1971 to 1972 and was awarded the Bronze Star for his service.

Mecca has been a consultant to substance abuse programs in Australia, Southeast Asia, the Middle East, Europe, India, China, and the United

States. He has written twelve books and edited numerous publications on self-esteem, substance abuse treatment and prevention, and mentoring.

A physical fitness enthusiast, Mecca was a marathon runner and participated in two cross-country runs from San Francisco to Washington, D.C. He has also competed in the Ironman Triathlon in Hawaii and completed fifty marathons. The number of golf rounds and tournaments is still being tallied.

Andy married the girl of his dreams, Kate, and they have been together for forty years. They live in Tiburon, California, and Hualalai, Hawaii.